HOME BUYING

FROM **MORTGAGES** AND **THE MLS** TO **MAKING THE OFFER** AND **MOVING IN,** YOUR ESSENTIAL GUIDE TO **BUYING YOUR FIRST HOME**

101

HOME BUYING

101

FROM **MORTGAGES** AND **THE MLS** TO **MAKING THE OFFER** AND **MOVING IN**, YOUR ESSENTIAL GUIDE TO **BUYING YOUR FIRST HOME**

JON GOREY

ADAMS MEDIA

NEW YORK LONDON TORONTO SYDNEY NEW DELHI

Adams Media
An Imprint of Simon & Schuster, Inc.
100 Technology Center Drive
Stoughton, Massachusetts 02072

First Adams Media hardcover edition February 2022

ADAMS MEDIA and colophon are trademarks of Simon & Schuster.

For information about special discounts for bulk purchases, please contact Simon & Schuster Special Sales at 1-866-506-1949 or business@simonandschuster.com.

The Simon & Schuster Speakers Bureau can bring authors to your live event. For more information or to book an event contact the Simon & Schuster Speakers Bureau at 1-866-248-3049 or visit our website at www.simonspeakers.com.

Manufactured in the United States of America

3 2023

Library of Congress Cataloging-in-Publication Data has been applied for.

ISBN 978-1-5072-1740-5
ISBN 978-1-5072-1741-2 (ebook)

CONTENTS

INTRODUCTION

Buying your first home is a big deal. Whether you're thinking of purchasing a single-family house, a condo, or even a multi-family property, buying a home marks a major financial commitment, an emotional milestone, and a powerful investment in your future.

Homeownership can help you create more than just memories and a sense of place—it can help you build lasting, multigenerational wealth for you and your family. And yet, even though everyone needs a place to call home, purchasing property isn't something you're likely to do very often in your life—maybe a handful of times at most.

That's one reason the home buying process can feel so exciting and so daunting at the same time. You're about to take a big, unfamiliar step, literally opening a door to a new world of possibility. It's not a step to take lightly, and getting the keys to that door won't be easy: It will demand thousands of dollars, head-spinning contracts, and more math than you'd probably care to know. The home you buy, and where it's located, can have an outsized impact on your life for years to come. Simply put, there's a lot riding on this decision.

But don't fear: As momentous and mystifying as all that sounds, *Home Buying 101* will get you ready to meet this high-stakes challenge with confidence. It'll help you determine whether you're ready to buy a home—and if not, what it will take to get you there. You'll learn practical strategies for saving up a down payment, or even avoiding one altogether, and boosting your credit score to make yourself mortgage-ready. You'll find out why a home's location is so important, and how to gauge the personality and livability of a community. You'll gain an understanding of essential home systems, from water heaters to wiring, and how to evaluate their condition. You'll be introduced to the key concepts and players involved in a real estate transaction, and learn about working with home professionals and negotiating an offer.

In addition, *Home Buying 101* answers such questions as:

- How much house can you afford?
- Why do you need a Realtor?
- What are points?
- What are closing costs, and who pays them?
- Why and when should you lock your interest rate?

From your first open house to the moment you cross the threshold as a new homeowner, *Home Buying 101* will take you step by step through the process so you'll be better prepared to make the purchase of a lifetime.

Chapter 1

Are You Ready to Buy a Home?

You're about to embark on a momentous journey. If all goes well, by the time you finish reading this book you may literally be in a different location, even if it's just across town.

But you're in for an emotional odyssey as well. Buying your first home is one of the most exciting things you can do—a whole new world of possibilities. It may also push your budgetary boundaries to the breaking point and test your patience and resilience. You are bound to face moments of disappointment and worry along the way—together with relief, excitement, and immense pride and satisfaction. So: Are you ready?

WHY BUY A HOME?

Define Your Dreams

Owning a home has long been considered a cornerstone of the American Dream—one that doesn't appear to be going away anytime soon. A recent survey of teens and young adults in Generation Z revealed that 86 percent plan to own a home one day.

So there's a good chance homeownership is something you've always wanted and imagined for yourself. But as you begin the exciting process of turning that vision into reality, it's worth reflecting on the contours of your particular homeownership dream.

The enduring image of "home" is that of a single-family house (an increasingly larger one) with a white picket fence outside. But that version of the American Dream is hardly the only one available, and it may not fit your wants, goals, or circumstances. So don't force yourself into someone else's idea of what "home" should look like. Think about what *you* want from a home.

Home is what and where you make it. It can be a cabin in the woods or a condo in a high-rise building downtown. It can be a place to set down roots and make lasting memories, or part of a long-term investment strategy (or both). Buying a home is your chance to define your dreams.

Most Buyers Would Prefer a House to a Condo—If They Can Afford One

Nine out of ten home buyers (89 percent) said they would prefer a single-family home with a backyard to a condo closer to their workplace, according to a 2019 study by the real estate brokerage Redfin.

REASONS TO BUY A HOME

Homeownership isn't just about achieving a personal life goal, however. There are some very practical reasons to purchase a home, and they boil down to two important considerations.

Take Control of (and Pride in) Your Housing Situation

In some ways, renting affords great freedom: You can bounce around to find a better deal, move back in with family to cut expenses if you lose a job, or even sublet your apartment if you want to skip town for the summer (if your lease agreement allows it).

At the same time, you're at the mercy of the market and your landlord. Your rent can spiral higher and higher each year, whether or not there have been any upgrades to your apartment. And if your landlord decides to sell the building, you may have to find a new place to live on fairly short notice, no matter how much you like your existing home.

Homeownership pins you down to some degree, but it also puts you in the driver's seat. As rents rise, your mortgage payment will pretty much stay the same (assuming you've locked in your interest rate), aside from potential increases in your property tax bill.

Owning your home also puts you in charge of your future. You can stay in your home as long as you like, sell it when you're ready to move, and, unless you stop paying your mortgage, nobody's going to force you to find a new place to live.

When it all comes down to it, there's something innately fulfilling about being the king or queen of your castle, so to speak. Most homeowners report feelings of self-improvement and emotional investment after buying a home, as well as a deep sense of pride and satisfaction.

Start Building Equity

Over the past century, homeownership has been the leading engine of wealth creation among middle-class Americans. It's such a powerful tool for generational wealth building, in fact, that much of the vast racial wealth gap in our country today can be traced to policies such as twentieth-century redlining practices, which denied Black Americans the same home buying opportunities that white Americans enjoyed.

But despite what you might see on house-flipping shows, owning a home is not a get-rich-quick scheme—even if it seems that way when nearby homes inspire bidding wars. Hot markets can cool down fast: During the Great Recession of 2007–2009, many people, including both ordinary homeowners and savvy investors, lost a lot of money on their homes when prices cratered.

The real wealth-building magic of home ownership is very simple: It's a forced savings vehicle.

We all need a place to live, and when you own your home, much of the "rent" you pay goes to your future self. As you pay down the principal of your mortgage, and as the home appreciates in value, you gain more and more equity in your home.

What Is Home Equity?

Equity is your ownership stake in your home. It's the difference between what you owe on it and what it's worth. For example, if you buy a $350,000 house with a $300,000 mortgage, your initial equity stake is $50,000. If, after a few years, you've paid down your mortgage balance to $250,000, and your home has appreciated in value to $400,000, now you have $150,000 in home equity.

Home equity is a cornerstone of middle-class wealth. Many homeowners later borrow against their home equity to make other investments in their financial future, whether it's paying for college, starting a business, or funding a remodel that further increases their home's value.

While real estate is generally a very good investment, and home values have outperformed inflation over the long term, it's not a guaranteed money maker. But that's almost beside the point. Because even if your home's value somehow *never* goes up—even if it decreases in value, as many homes did during the Great Recession—if you simply pay down the mortgage, after thirty years you'll have a free place to live. (Okay, *almost* free: You'll still owe taxes and insurance, which we'll discuss next.)

WHAT IT MEANS (AND COSTS) TO BE A HOMEOWNER

If You Don't Have a Go-To Plumber, You Soon Will

The leap from renting to owning your own home is a big one. In a sense, it's like leaving a salaried job to be your own boss: You're taking on more work and responsibility in exchange for more control and the potential for bigger financial gains.

But here's another way to think about it: Consider the difference between playing with your three-year-old nephew for an afternoon and raising a toddler yourself. Both can be wonderful experiences—but in very different ways.

Babysitting can be challenging, to be sure. In between the giggles and hugs, there may be a tantrum or a scraped knee, and you may have to pay for movie tickets or ice cream cones. But when it comes down to it, you're off the hook once you bring the kid back to his folks.

His parents, meanwhile, are the ones who might be woken up at 3 a.m. if the little guy has a nightmare, who may themselves have stress dreams about his safety, and who probably pay hundreds of dollars a month for his healthcare, food, and preschool. Yet most parents would no doubt tell you their child is the best thing that's ever happened to them.

Like raising a child, owning a home typically inspires immense pride and joy. But because you're so invested, it can also be a source of nonstop worry and ongoing expense.

THE BUCK STOPS HERE

As a homeowner, you're the boss. That means you can paint your walls whatever color you like without asking anyone's permission. Heck, you can even knock some of them down if you really want to (but please ask a licensed contractor first).

It means that, not only can you get a dog but you can install a fence in the yard and cut a big hole in the back door to install a pet door. And you're the one who will reap the resale rewards of any home improvements you make.

But unless you buy a condo in a full-service building, it also means that when the shower turns cold on a chilly winter morning, you're the one who has to hire and pay for a plumber to replace the hot water heater. You're the person on call when something leaks, whether it's the kitchen sink or the roof. When the refrigerator or the oven breaks, you're the one suddenly spending hundreds of dollars at the hardware store on a Tuesday when you should be at work.

How Long Do Appliances Last?

An older study by the National Association of Home Builders estimated the life expectancy of various home components from furnaces to flooring. Among the shorter-lived appliances were dishwashers, which last about nine years on average; washers (ten years); and water heaters (ten to eleven years). Refrigerators and dryers could be expected to last thirteen years. A wood deck ought to make it to twenty years, while wood floors can be expected to last a lifetime.

THE COSTS OF HOMEOWNERSHIP

While house hunting, you'll understandably focus on your monthly mortgage payment and how much home that budget can buy (something we'll cover in Chapter 3). But there are other expenses you need to prepare for too.

Home Insurance and Property Taxes

These costs are lumped on top of your monthly mortgage payment or included in the condo fee, so hopefully you're already aware of them; most online mortgage calculators include estimated values to help you set your budget, but they will vary based on your home's value and location.

The average homeowner's insurance policy costs north of $1,300 a year, according to *Bankrate*. Meanwhile, the Tax Foundation estimated that annual property tax rates ranged from 0.3 percent to 2.21 percent of a home's assessed value in 2020. And unlike the fixed portion of your mortgage that goes to the bank, taxes and insurance premiums will generally rise as time goes on.

Water, Sewer, and Utilities

Water, of course, is almost always included in rent; sometimes even heat or electric service is too. These utilities may be included in your condo fee, but one way or another, you'll be paying for all of them as a homeowner, in addition to your mortgage.

Maintenance

Experts suggest budgeting 1 percent of your home's value a year for maintenance—on a $400,000 home, that's a whopping $4,000 a year.

That might seem a ludicrous price for basic upkeep—which you might imagine includes, say, painting the deck every few years or getting the gutters cleaned. But the fact is, most home systems only last about thirty years, and if you spread out their replacement costs, they add up.

Over the course of fifteen years, for example, you might have to replace the roof ($10,000) at some point, the furnace or boiler ($5,000), and maybe the water heater or refrigerator too. Spread out over time, and that's over $1,000 a year right there, even before you pay for a chimney sweep or septic clean-out.

Time

Owning a home—especially a house with a yard—will also eat into your free time. There's grass to mow, leaves to rake, snow to shovel. There are drains to unclog, lights to fix, railings to repaint. And there's no landlord to do any of it for you.

You might find a soothing sense of satisfaction in this work, but there's no question that it will demand some of your weekends. As one home inspector said, only half-jokingly, "If you're buying an older single-family house, sell your golf clubs, because you've got a new hobby now."

HOME BUYING READINESS CHECKLIST

Are You Ready to Buy a Home?

Between the benefits, responsibilities, and financial obligations, the decision to buy a home is a big one. And it's not for everyone—at least, not at all times. Ask yourself these questions to determine whether you're ready to buy a home right now.

Are You Prepared to Stay in One Place for Four Years or More?

Most experts say you should plan to own a home you buy for at least three or four years, and longer if possible, to hedge against economic risks. Homes are generally a safe investment—but that's over the long term. In the short term, housing prices can fall just like the stock market. And it's a lot more tedious, time-consuming, and expensive to sell a home than a share of Apple stock.

It's Expensive to Sell a Home

Realtor commissions average more than 5 percent of a home's sale price—and they're paid entirely by the seller in most cases. That means you need to sell your home for at least 5 percent more than what you paid for it just to break even. So unless your home has had time to appreciate in value, you may lose money when you go to sell. Meanwhile, even if the home *has* risen in value, you may need to pay capital gains tax on any home sale profits if you've lived in the property for less than two years.

Do You Have a Down Payment and an Emergency Fund Saved Up?

While there are first-time home buyer loans that don't require the traditional 20 percent down payment, even the more generous programs generally require *some* down payment, often around 3 percent to 5 percent of the purchase price. On a $400,000 home, that's $12,000 or more. In addition, most lenders want you to have enough cash left over to handle emergency repairs or to make a few months of mortgage payments if you should lose your job.

If you don't have that much in savings, you're not alone—it's the biggest obstacle for first-time home buyers everywhere. Turn to Chapter 2 for tips on saving for a down payment.

How Much of Your Monthly Income Goes to Debt, Like Student Loans and Car Payments?

When you apply for a mortgage, lenders will look at how much debt you're obligated to pay each month—including your potential mortgage—and compare that to your gross monthly income. This is called your *debt-to-income ratio*, or DTI, and they want it to be 43 percent or less.

If you earn $5,000 a month before taxes, for example, and $1,000 of that goes to various debts—such as car payments, student loans, and minimum credit card payments—that represents a 20 percent debt-to-income ratio. Add a $1,500 mortgage to the mix, and your debts will amount to $2,500 each month, for a debt-to-income ratio of 50 percent; most lenders won't approve that loan. You'll either need to make more money, take out a smaller home loan, or pay off your credit cards or car loan before you apply for a mortgage. (See Chapter 3 for tips on paying down debt.)

Is Your Credit Score 620 or Better?

It's possible to secure a mortgage with a lower credit score, but you'll generally have a harder time gaining approval. Even with a score in the mid-600s, you may have to pay higher interest rates or fees than someone with a better score. That might not sound like a big deal, but half a percentage point difference on a $300,000 mortgage can cost you an extra $30,000 in interest over the life of the loan. It's worth trying to get your credit score into the 700s before you buy a home. Find tips for raising your credit score in Chapter 3.

Have You Been in the Same Job or Line of Work for Two Years or More?

When it comes to your employment situation, lenders like to see steadiness. If you haven't been in the same job for the past two years, you'll need to provide prior job and salary history as well. Qualifying for a mortgage can be particularly tricky for independent contractors and small business owners; they need to provide two years of tax returns that show a solid income history.

Are You Prepared to Stay Rational and Levelheaded Through Some Emotional Setbacks?

Home buying is a financial investment, but it's also an emotional roller coaster. To get to the point where you're prepared to offer hundreds of thousands of dollars for a home, you have to really fall in love with the place—and yet your offer might lose out to someone else's, leaving you crushed.

Finding the right home at the right price can take months and will almost certainly test your patience. Be prepared to suffer some disappointment, but try not to let the resulting frustration cloud your financial judgment or strain your relationship if you're searching with a partner.

IT'S OKAY TO KEEP RENTING

You're Not "Throwing Money Away"

If you answered no to any of those questions, you might not be 100 percent ready to buy a home right now. And that's okay. Most first-time home buyers aren't. (Who has $20,000 or more just lying around?) It might take time, but don't worry; you'll learn how to get ready in the chapters ahead, starting with strategies for saving up a down payment.

But know this: It's perfectly okay to continue renting or living with family members if you're not ready to purchase a home just yet.

Stepping back from the house hunt doesn't mean that you'll never buy a home. It just means you'll be better prepared when you do. In fact, holding off and renting for another year—and getting your home purchase right the first time—could be the difference between owning your dream home five years from now and feeling trapped in a home you can't afford.

It can be hard to sit on the sidelines, though. A buzzing housing market and spiraling home prices can create a feeling of urgency—like you're late for the bus, and you can see it pulling away (with your friends or coworkers aboard). The FOMO is real.

But although people may say you're "throwing money away" every year that you don't buy a home, renting has real advantages—notably, the freedom to pick up and move in pursuit of a more lucrative job opportunity (or just for fun). In fact, some financial advisors recommend renting, insisting that you can ultimately earn more money by investing your down payment and other saved costs in the stock market instead of in a high-upkeep home. If you're on an upward trajectory early in your career, you never know when the job of a lifetime might open up a thousand miles away; as a renter, it's a lot easier to break a lease and pursue such life-changing opportunities.

Even if you have no intention of moving across the country, renting allows you to audition different communities or neighborhoods without committing your life's savings to them. And depending on the building, you may be able to enjoy perks like a pool, roof deck, or a yard without having to deal with the headaches or costs of maintenance.

Living with family members, meanwhile, can certainly test the patience of everyone involved. But it could be a good chance for you to offer much-needed companionship or around-the-house assistance to an older family member or to strengthen relationships with your parents, siblings, or cousins. Meanwhile, even if you chip in rent, you may have an opportunity to save a bit on housing costs, so you can sock away more money for an eventual down payment.

The fact is, you're better off waiting until you're truly ready to buy a home than prematurely jumping into a mortgage that will overextend your finances. Homeownership is a tried-and-true path toward wealth creation, but it can also lead to serious financial strain, stress, and hardship if you're not on firm financial footing.

Nearly ten million American households lost their homes to foreclosure between 2006 and 2014, largely due to predatory lending practices that lured home buyers into mortgages they couldn't sustain. Those homeowners were forced out of their homes and bore the scars of the default on their credit reports for years to come.

A Seven-Year Curse

Even a single missed mortgage payment can quickly sink your credit score. But a foreclosure remains on your credit report for seven years and will generally disqualify you from taking out a mortgage for at least three years or more after the fact.

New laws require lenders to be far more cautious, fair, and straightforward when writing mortgages today. They must prove a borrower meets "ability to pay" requirements, and shady subprime loan practices such as balloon-payment loans are a thing of the past. But it's still possible for well-qualified borrowers to get overstretched—especially if life throws you a curveball like a job loss, divorce, or health crisis.

Even as home values surged in 2020, more than three million Americans were severely underwater on their mortgage in the fourth quarter, according to ATTOM Data Solutions—meaning they owed a lot more on their mortgages than what their homes were actually worth. In a situation like that, there's rarely a good way out. Best-case scenario: You keep paying your mortgage, more or less stuck with that home until its value goes up or you've paid the balance down. If you can't keep up with your mortgage payments, and you can't sell your home for at least as much as you owe on it, you'll be left paying some of the difference when you sell—money you probably don't have—or enduring the foreclosure process.

Let's be clear: That's not how the vast majority of homeownership experiences go. But it is a possibility, and not one you want to invite on yourself if you can avoid it. You're looking to buy a home, not an albatross around your neck. So it's worth waiting until you feel ready.

"Waiting" to buy doesn't have to mean spinning your wheels in a holding pattern, however. Whether you need a few more months or a few more years to prepare, if you know you'd like to buy a home one day, now is the time to start saving, to start learning, and to start researching the home buying process, so that when you are fully prepared, you can pounce.

Chapter 2

Figuring Out the Down Payment

You've probably seen commercials where auto dealerships offer to sell you a new car or truck with "No money down!" Unfortunately, buying a home almost always requires a down payment, and coming up with that chunk of cash is typically the biggest hurdle for first-time home buyers.

In this chapter, we'll look at how much you may need to scrape together for a down payment, and some savings strategies to help you reach that target. But we'll also explore some of the first-time home buyer loans and assistance programs that can make it possible to buy a home with a smaller down payment—or even none at all.

WHAT'S A DOWN PAYMENT, AND HOW MUCH DO YOU NEED TO SAVE UP?

A 20 Percent Deposit Is Ideal but by No Means Necessary

The biggest hurdle most first-time home buyers face is coming up with a down payment. This is a cash deposit on the house that essentially protects the lender should you default on the loan.

The down payment reduces a lender's risk in two ways. Most obviously, it builds in a bit of financial cushion in the event that the home's value decreases. But it also ensures that you as the home buyer are more deeply invested in the home—that you and the lender share a common interest and stake in its condition, and you're thus more likely to take good care of it.

The standard, traditional down payment is 20 percent of the purchase price. On a $350,000 home, that's an astounding $70,000 in cash. You probably don't have that kind of money lying around, *and that's okay.* One reason many buyers do is because they're selling their existing home for more than they paid for it—they're able to use the home equity they've built up as a down payment on their next house.

What if you don't already own a house to sell? A number of first-time home buyer programs require no more than a 5 percent or even 3 percent down payment. As well, active-duty service members, military veterans, and rural home buyers can sometimes access $0 down payment loans through the US Department of Veterans Affairs or the US Department of Agriculture. We'll cover some of those federal loan options later in this chapter.

What's more, as with so much else in life, the "ideal scenario" doesn't exactly square with reality. The median down payment in 2019 was 12 percent, according to an exhaustive survey of recent home buyers conducted by the National Association of Realtors—nowhere near a full 20 percent. Among first-time buyers, the median down payment was even lower, at just 6 percent. You absolutely don't need a full 20 percent down payment to purchase a home.

That said, you should still aim to put down as big a down payment as possible. It doesn't have to be a fifth of the purchase price, but strive for 10 percent, or even 5 percent. On that same $350,000 house, that puts your target at about $17,500 to $35,000. At a bare minimum, you'll probably need to save up $10,500, or 3 percent of the purchase price.

The larger your down payment, the sooner you'll build up real equity in your home, and the more manageable your monthly mortgage will be. With a $10,500 down payment, for example, the mortgage payment on that $350,000 home would be $1,621 a month, assuming a 4 percent interest rate on a thirty-year, fixed-rate mortgage. By comparison, putting down $35,000 would yield a monthly payment of $1,504, saving you more than $110 a month for the next thirty years. A larger down payment will generally help you qualify for lower interest rates and better loan terms as well.

The more you can save up as a down payment, the more options you'll give yourself. Extra cash can extend your price range without impacting your monthly budget. It can make your offer more attractive to sellers or help you overcome any last-minute hiccups with the home sale. And let's be honest: It never hurts to have more money on hand, so it's not as if the savings will go to waste if you don't need to put the entire amount toward a home. Whatever's left over could help pay for a kitchen or bathroom remodel or cover the cost of a new roof or furnace.

Because lenders view a low-down-payment mortgage as a riskier proposition, they generally require borrowers to pay private mortgage insurance, or PMI, if they put less than 20 percent down. PMI is something of a mixed bag. Without it, millions of buyers would be unable to purchase a home. And yet, it feels like a lousy deal. It's insurance that you have to pay for, but it doesn't protect you—it protects the bank.

How Much Does PMI Add to Your Mortgage Payment?

The cost of private mortgage insurance (PMI) will vary, but you can expect to pay $30 to $70 a month per $100,000 borrowed, according to mortgage giant Freddie Mac.

Paying PMI is practically a matter of course for many first-time home buyers, but it's still an added cost in the early years of your mortgage, and the closer you can get to a full 20 percent down payment, the less you'll ultimately pay in PMI. (We'll cover PMI in greater detail in Chapter 4.)

Coming up with a down payment isn't easy—but it's not impossible, either, especially if you give yourself plenty of time. In the next section, we'll look at some potential strategies for amassing a home deposit, from extreme budgeting to local grants and interest-free loans for first-time home buyers.

SAVING FOR A DOWN PAYMENT

Cut Expenses and Stash Your Cash

So how the heck do you come up with $10,500 to $35,000 or more in savings? Time is perhaps your best ally in this goal, so start saving early. Here we'll look at a range of techniques to help you sock away enough cash for a down payment, from aggressive budgeting to part-time side hustles.

AUTOMATE YOUR SAVINGS

First things first: Set up a high-interest savings account, or a folder within your current bank account, specifically designated for your down payment. (Some banks will even award you with a cash sign-up bonus if you open a new account with them, so keep an eye out for promotional offers.)

Then, set up an automatic transfer from your checking account into savings—as much as you think you can safely spare without bouncing rent checks or risking overdraft fees. Moving $100 a week will net you $5,200 by year's end, but any amount—even just $10 a week—is better than nothing and can help you build momentum toward your goal.

If you get paid via direct deposit at work, you can also ask your payroll department to split your paycheck between the two accounts, so that 90 percent goes into checking, for example, and 10 percent is dumped directly into your down payment fund.

Automating is an incredibly effective saving technique, because you're less likely to spend (or miss) money you don't see. If a portion of your paycheck never makes it into your checking account, it's just not there to spend, quietly forcing you to be more careful with your money.

SET ASIDE ALL "BONUS" MONEY

Starting right now, decide that any "found" money or other cash windfall will go straight into your down payment fund. This includes holiday and birthday gifts—even that twenty bucks from your aunt— plus any work bonuses or tax refunds.

This takes some real discipline, as most of us would rather splurge on a celebratory night out or vacation after coming into unexpected cash (if it's not already earmarked for last month's rent or an overdue credit card bill). But the average tax refund was $2,535 in 2019, and that could go a long way fast toward bolstering your down payment fund.

PAY DOWN HIGH-INTEREST DEBT

That said, if you're carrying a high credit card balance—and paying $100 a month or more in interest on it—that could be a good target for your tax refund.

Paying down credit card debt can make you better qualified for a mortgage since it will boost your credit score and improve your debt-to-income ratio—two important considerations among lenders. It will also reduce the amount you're paying in exorbitant interest charges each month, money that could be going to your down payment fund instead.

However, in the short term, this does mean diverting potential savings away from your down payment fund. Aggressively paying off credit card debt is a longer-term strategy, but a powerful one. Once you get the balance to zero, don't take your foot off the gas: Take whatever money you were paying toward your credit card each month and start putting that amount into your down payment fund. When you finally go from, say, *paying* $400 a month (much of that money going toward double-digit interest rates) to *saving* $400 a month, it's an incredible turnaround—like intercepting a pass in the end zone and running it back for a touchdown.

CUT YOUR MONTHLY EXPENSES AND SAVE THE DIFFERENCE

Serious savers know that cutting costs is where you can make the most progress the fastest. Look at your monthly bills and consider what services you could live without for a while. These cuts don't have to be permanent; just go without until you save enough for a down payment—though you might discover that you can get by just fine without them.

Start with discretionary services, such as your cable TV or streaming subscriptions. If you're still paying full freight for cable in this day and age, look at cord-cutting options that free you from cable services. Better yet, if you live near a major city, buy a digital antenna to receive live local broadcasts. You may be surprised by how much great content is available for free, and in high definition, over the airwaves. If you've already cut cable, take an inventory of the streaming services you subscribe to. Do you need all of them? Drop the ones you don't use much.

Look at other monthly expenses, big and small: Can you cancel or pause your gym membership for a few months and work out at home or outside? Are you subscribed to magazines you never find time to read? Definitely hit pause on any monthly goodie-box subscriptions while you're trying to amass a down payment.

Set a Streaming Rotation

One popular, simple money-saving strategy is to binge-watch content from one streaming service for a couple of months, and then cancel and move on to another service, instead of paying for all of them all the time.

Next, see if you can save money on essential expenses. Are you not driving as much now, because you've been working from home? Call your car insurance company and ask for a discount. (Or, if it's been a while, shop around for a new insurer.) Have you checked your cell phone plan lately? Your carrier may have new, cheaper options available, or you could investigate a lower-cost provider.

Then comes the important part: *Don't let these savings evaporate.* Increase your automatic savings transfer by whatever amount of money you're able to trim from your ongoing expenses. Your checking account won't know the difference.

Practice Money Mindfulness

Not all spending is so regimented, of course. So make a critical, Marie Kondo–inspired review of your bank and credit card statements from the last few months. Look for charges that, in retrospect, didn't really bring you joy.

Did you ever read those books you bought, or are they still sitting on the shelf? Sure, it was on sale, but did you really need that new sweater? Do you even remember what you bought for $23.79 at that highway rest stop? Look for patterns of thoughtless spending, and vow to be more mindful with your money.

COOK AT HOME

Yes, after more than a year spent in varying degrees of coronavirus lockdown, we're all a little tired of eating at home. But if you started cooking for yourself more often during the pandemic, keep up the habit. If you're the type who ordinarily goes out to dinner often, even cutting back on just one night out a week can add up quickly.

If you really want to turbocharge your food savings, combine home cooking with more careful grocery-shopping habits. Plan out your meals for the week, and shop for just those ingredients (with a list) to avoid impulse purchases. Subbing in a meal like beans and rice for a meat-based dinner once in a while can be a healthy way to save money too. And buy generic or store-brand items as a default. This may only save you 25 to 50 cents at a time, but when you multiply that by twenty or more items a week, fifty-two weeks a year, it adds up to $250 to $500 in savings from a single, simple—almost effortless—change.

SELL SOME STUFF

If you're successful in buying a home, you're going to be moving before long. Why not get a jump on decluttering and start cleaning out closets and selling some things?

If you have a lot of random, low-value items—kids' clothes, toys, books, DVDs, video games, knickknacks—then holding a yard sale is probably your best bet. For higher-value items, such as collectibles, designer clothes, and toys that hold their resale value well (such as LEGOs), it's often worth selling them individually online. You can list items on general resale sites, such as *eBay* or *Facebook Marketplace*, or on niche sites, such as *Poshmark* or *thredUP* for clothes.

PICK UP A SIDE HUSTLE

However you feel about the tech-and-capitalism cocktail that is the modern gig economy, there's no denying that it's given us a way to make some quick side cash. Even if you just pick up four to six hours a week—a Saturday afternoon, or a couple of weeknights after work—you can earn an extra $50 to $100 a week and have the funds deposited directly into your down payment account.

If you've got a reliable car and can pass a background check, you can shop for and deliver groceries through Shipt, Instacart, or Postmates; pick up take-out through DoorDash; or shuttle passengers around as an Uber or Lyft driver. You can pick up babysitting gigs through Sittercity or Care.com, walk dogs through Wag! or Rover, or perform odd jobs on TaskRabbit or Fiverr.

There are plenty of other options too; see which services are most popular in your area and offer the best mix of pay potential and schedule flexibility. Just be aware of two hidden costs: You'll be using more gas and putting more wear and tear on your vehicle if you drive, and you'll owe some income tax on your earnings later (which isn't withheld automatically, since you'll be paid as an independent contractor).

OTHER DOWN PAYMENT SOURCES

How to Tap Retirement Accounts and Handle Cash Gifts

While getting into a good savings routine will serve you well in life—for long after you buy your first home—there are some faster ways to come up with big chunks of down payment money, if they're available to you.

TAP YOUR RETIREMENT SAVINGS

Most financial planners advise against this strategy, because so many Americans are woefully underprepared for retirement. However, you may be able to pull money out of a workplace or Individual Retirement Account (IRA) and use it toward your down payment without paying the harsh 10 percent penalty that the Internal Revenue Service typically charges for early withdrawals taken before age fifty-nine and a half.

The most flexible account for this purpose is the Roth IRA, which allows you to withdraw contributions—that is, the money you've deposited into the account over the years—at any time, for any purpose, without a penalty. If you've had a Roth IRA for more than five years, you can also pull out an additional $10,000 in earnings (i.e., investment gains) to be used toward a first-time home purchase.

With a traditional IRA, you can similarly withdraw up to $10,000 to put toward your first home (including renovations), without paying the 10 percent penalty. However, you will have to pay ordinary income taxes on the withdrawal when you file your taxes the following year—just as if you got a $10,000 bonus at work (except in this case, it's your future self awarding you the cash).

Unfortunately, common workplace retirement accounts, such as 401(k)s and 403(b)s, offer no such exemption. You can take money out of these accounts in the event of a "financial hardship," but you'll pay both income taxes *and* a 10 percent early withdrawal penalty, which makes it a pretty terrible deal.

However, there is a workaround: If you have an old 401(k) from a previous job, you can roll that over into an IRA. This doesn't cost anything, but it generally takes a phone call and a few weeks' time. Once the account has been converted to a traditional IRA, you could take advantage of the early-withdrawal exemption for buying your first home.

Lastly, you can actually loan yourself money from your 401(k), up to half the account's value or $50,000, whichever is less. You won't have to pay taxes or a penalty on this money, but you will have to pay back the loan, plus interest. The good news is, that interest is going toward your own retirement. The bad news is, this new debt obligation may work against you when it comes time to qualify for a mortgage: Borrowing $10,000 at a 6 percent interest rate, for example, will saddle you with a monthly payment of $193 for the next five years, adding to your debt-to-income ratio. So make sure it doesn't tip the scales on your debt burden, and that you can easily afford the repayment schedule.

Rules and limits for 401(k) loans can vary by employer, but generally, you'll have five years to pay yourself back, with interest, unless you leave the company—in which case, you may need to pay off the remaining balance immediately or face an early withdrawal penalty.

Lending Yourself a Down Payment

Since you're borrowing from your (future) self, the worst that can happen if you fail to pay back a 401(k) loan is that the loan turns into a regular early withdrawal: You'll pay the 10 percent early withdrawal penalty plus ordinary income taxes and miss out on investment growth in your retirement account, but the default won't impact your credit report.

GIFTS FROM FAMILY MEMBERS

You'll want to be tactful and respectful about it, of course, but you can also ask family members for some financial help. If your parents or grandparents own their home, they've likely experienced a surge in their home equity over the past few years—so they may be able and willing to chip in toward your home buying dream.

You need to be careful with big cash gifts, however. If $10,000 suddenly materializes in your bank account two weeks before you apply for a mortgage, your lender will want to know where it came from. This generally applies to any large, irregular deposit to your account within sixty days of your mortgage application.

Ideally, it's good to get this type of financial assistance squared away months before you need it. Otherwise, in addition to their generous financial support, your family member will need to provide a signed letter for the mortgage lender stating that the money is, in fact, a gift, with no expectation of repayment or ownership stake in the home. (That's not to say you can't repay your relative later on if you'd like. But the lender wants to make sure you're not beholden to another creditor, even a familial one—the bank wants to be your top financial priority.)

The letter should include:

- Your family member's name, contact information, and relationship to you
- The dollar amount and date of the transfer
- The address of the property being purchased
- A statement, signed by both of you, that no repayment or ownership stake is expected

Since it's a gift, you won't have to pay taxes on the money (though you may feel obligated to be extra nice next Thanksgiving). Your relative, meanwhile, only needs to report a gift in excess of $15,000, the current gift tax exclusion as of 2021. (Even then, they should only owe tax on the amount above $15,000—but check with an accountant or tax professional, of course.)

LOW- OR NO-DOWN-PAYMENT MORTGAGES AND DOWN PAYMENT ASSISTANCE

Maybe You Don't Need to Save That Much After All?

For a lot of people with good credit and a stable job, saving a full down payment is the only thing standing in the way of homeownership. Policymakers recognize that reality, so there are many federal and state-sponsored mortgages that require little or even no down payment on a primary residence. Most are for first-time buyers only—but not all of them. Some state and local programs, meanwhile, offer down payment grants or interest-free loans to first-time buyers.

LOW-DOWN-PAYMENT MORTGAGES

Low- or moderate-income buyers can access a number of different first-time home buyer loans at the federal and state level, with varying eligibility requirements and limits. In general, these low- or no-down-payment mortgages can't exceed the conforming loan limit, which in 2021 ranges from $548,250 up to $822,375 in high-cost areas. Most have other restrictions, too, such as income limits, and require borrowers to complete a home buying education course. Here's a look at some of the most common options.

- **VA loans:** Active-duty military, veterans, and surviving spouses can finance a home purchase with as little as $0 down payment through the Department of Veterans Affairs, and you don't even have to be a first-time home buyer. Since VA loans are directly backed by the federal government, borrowers without great credit may also qualify. You won't have to pay private mortgage insurance with a VA loan, but they do require a one-time, upfront fee (which can typically be financed into the loan).

- **USDA loans:** Buyers in rural areas can also secure a $0 down payment mortgage backed by the government, courtesy of the US Department of Agriculture. USDA-guaranteed loans are available to low- and moderate-income buyers alike, provided they're purchasing a primary residence in an eligible community (some of which are only twenty miles outside of a big city); you can check USDA.gov to find out whether a town or specific address qualifies. Like VA loans, there's no private mortgage insurance required, but USDA loans do have an upfront one-time fee and a smaller annual fee paid monthly.

- **Fannie Mae and Freddie Mac:** These two quasi-governmental agencies own most of the residential mortgages in America, and they set the standards used by lenders all over the country. Both agencies now allow home loans with as little as 3 percent down. Fannie Mae's HomeReady Mortgage and Freddie Mac's Home Possible loan are both available to low-income buyers—including repeat buyers—with credit scores as low as 620, provided borrowers meet debt, income, and other requirements. Both agencies also offer a standard loan with a 3 percent down payment requirement to first-time buyers at any income level. You can apply for these mortgage products at virtually any lender.

- **FHA loans:** The Federal Housing Administration (FHA) offers a variety of government-backed mortgages, including loans for first-time buyers, fixer-uppers, and new construction. First-time buyers can qualify for a home loan with a 3.5 percent down payment and a credit score as low as 580, though the FHA has lower lending limits in some areas. Low-down-payment FHA borrowers must also pay mortgage insurance for the life of the loan, and FHA loans require a separate property inspection.

- **State housing finance agencies:** Every state has its own non-profit Housing Finance Agency (HFA), dedicated to meeting the affordable housing needs of its low- and moderate-income residents. These agencies generally offer first-time home buyer loans with affordable fixed rates, low-down-payment options, consumer education, and even, in some cases, down payment assistance, which we'll explain next.

Financing a Fixer-Upper with a Rehab Loan

With just a 3.5 percent down payment, qualified buyers can use an FHA 203(k) loan, often called a rehab or renovation loan, to finance the purchase of a fixer-upper and roll the costs of any needed renovations or repairs into the mortgage. These loans can't be used for "luxury" improvements, such as adding a swimming pool. But they can be used to fund basic cosmetic updates, essential repairs, energy-efficiency improvements, and upgrades to home systems like the plumbing or wiring. Buyers with better credit or higher income levels, meanwhile, can look into conventional rehab loans offered by Fannie Mae and Freddie Mac.

DOWN PAYMENT ASSISTANCE

Many cities, towns, counties, and states offer some form of down payment assistance to local first-time buyers who meet certain income restrictions and other criteria.

Often this assistance is in the form of a grant—a.k.a. free money—or a zero-interest loan, repaid only when you refinance or sell the home later. Other times the loan is forgivable, meaning that, as long as you use the property as your primary residence for a certain length of time, such as five or ten years, you won't have to pay back the debt.

There are almost always some strings attached—you generally must live in the home for a certain number of years, for example—but some programs are quite generous. MassHousing, the state housing finance agency in Massachusetts, now offers up to $15,000 in down payment assistance to first-time buyers, and up to $25,000 for buyers in certain cities. The city of Boston, meanwhile, offers its own down payment assistance program, a zero-interest loan of up to $30,000. And some of the new first-time buyer programs in Illinois offer up to $6,000 in down payment assistance (forgiven after five years), or up to $40,000 in student loan relief with a $5,000 loan toward a down payment.

Down payment assistance programs are generally only available to low- and middle-income buyers who haven't owned a home in the past three years and will use the property as their primary residence. Often you must kick in a minimum of $1,000 toward your down payment as well. But such programs exist in virtually every state and in hundreds of communities, so see what's available where you live.

Chapter 3

Readying Your Finances

It's never too early to start looking at homes for sale; every open house or online tour will help you sharpen your house-hunting senses. You'll start to understand what floor plans, features, and neighborhoods you like, which ones you don't, and what price trends are in your target area.

However, until you've actually taken a deep, honest look at your financial situation, any house hunting at this point is purely theoretical—like window shopping.

In this chapter, you'll see the numbers necessary to turn your daydreams into reality. You'll discover the key financial figures you need to understand, the benchmarks you'll need to meet to qualify for a home loan, and how to shore up your finances if you're not quite mortgage-ready.

HOW MUCH HOME CAN YOU AFFORD?

How to Find Your Target Price Range

If you're ready to get serious about buying a home, you need to figure out a realistic price range. Unless you've got a suitcase full of cash hidden somewhere, what you can afford generally boils down to how much a bank will let you borrow.

There are a lot of variables that determine how big a mortgage you'll qualify for and how much you can spend on a home. Some of these are outside of your control and can change by the day—such as mortgage interest rates, which move with the whims of the financial markets. Others are probably more rigid, such as your monthly income. Still others, like your credit score, can be changed and are directly under your control.

Here are two ways to determine your home buying budget, using the main factors that mortgage lenders will consider.

Method 1: Using an Online Calculator

You can find a number of good home affordability calculators online, but their results will only be as accurate as the information you supply. Here are the main data points you'll need to plug in:

- **Gross monthly income:** *Gross* just means "pretax," so divide your annual salary by 12. For example, someone earning $72,000 a year before taxes earns $6,000 a month. (Or you can multiply your weekly pretax pay by 52, and then divide that by 12.)
- **Monthly debt obligations:** Tally up any car payments, student loan bills, and minimum credit card payments that you pay each month.

- **Estimated down payment:** The more cash you have saved, the bigger your budget gets.
- **Your credit score range:** We'll talk about where to find your credit score and how to improve it later in this chapter.
- **Mortgage interest rate:** Most online calculators will fill in an estimated interest rate for you, but you can play around with those numbers and see just how big an impact they have on your monthly payment.
- **Property taxes and insurance:** Online calculators typically factor in estimated local property taxes and homeowner's insurance, too, both of which can vary by location.

One benefit of an online calculator is that it will spit out a home price that you can use as your price ceiling based on current interest rates. You can also adjust some of the variables to see what actions could help you reach a higher price tier. How much more could you afford if you paid off your car, for example, or if you scored a better interest rate? An online calculator can show you what each change could mean to your home budget in real terms.

Method 2: Using the 28 Percent Rule

Another way to quickly estimate how big a mortgage payment you can afford each month is to use 28 percent of your gross monthly income as a guide. By this rule, a couple earning a combined $120,000 a year, or $10,000 a month, should be able to afford a mortgage payment of about $2,800 a month, including taxes and home insurance.

All of this is academic, of course, until you take your financial documents to a lender. When you're ready, a loan officer will review your pay stubs, tax returns, bank statements, and other records to verify the financial information you provide, as well as perform a credit check.

If all goes well, you'll receive a preapproval letter, saying they're prepared to lend you a certain amount of money. This figure is based on current interest rates, so it can fluctuate a bit if rates change.

WHAT YOU CAN AFFORD VERSUS WHAT YOU'RE COMFORTABLE PAYING

Keep in mind that just because a bank thinks you can afford to buy a particular home, that doesn't necessarily mean that you can or should. You need to be comfortable with the monthly payment you're taking on and your ability to meet that obligation each month.

For example, what would happen if you lost your job? Could you cover the mortgage for a couple of months between savings and unemployment benefits? If you had to, could you take in a roommate or rent out the home for enough money to offset the mortgage payment? On the other hand, are you anticipating a promotion that would make even a high mortgage payment easier to manage a year from now?

Don't Forget Other Costs of Homeownership

Remember, owning a home can be expensive. Even a mortgage payment that's similar to your current monthly rent will typically come with some other less visible costs, from maintenance to water bills.

Only you know the answers to these questions. So even if your bank feels comfortable lending you a certain amount of money, make sure *you* feel okay with it too. That all starts with gaining a deeper, holistic understanding of your finances.

EVALUATING YOUR FINANCIAL SITUATION

View Yourself Through the Eyes of a Lender

Would you lend hundreds of thousands of dollars to a stranger if you didn't think they could pay you back? Of course not. That's why lenders carefully review a home buyer's financial stability and credit profile before offering them a home loan.

When a bank is deciding whether to approve your mortgage application, it's carefully evaluating your financial health—and the likelihood that you'll be able to repay the loan—based on a few benchmarks, which we'll look at in this section. Many Americans grimace when thinking about things like credit card debt or retirement savings (not to mention math in general). But understanding these metrics and how they relate to your mortgage application will help you get a better sense of your financial picture through the eyes of a lender.

Credit Score

Lenders use credit scores, imperfect as they are, as a shorthand measure of a borrower's creditworthiness. Your credit score is a numerical snapshot of your credit profile at a moment in time, which reflects things like your history of on-time (or late) bill payments.

There are multiple credit-scoring models available to banks, but the majority of lenders will use your FICO score. To qualify for a conventional mortgage, your FICO score ought to be 620 or better (on a scale of 300 to 850). Buyers with a score of 740 or higher will qualify for the best interest rates, but some mortgages, like FHA loans, are available to borrowers with scores as low as 580.

In short, the higher your credit score, the more (and better) mortgage options you'll have available to you. If your credit score is very low—due to a past bankruptcy or loan default, for example—you'll need to work on improving it over time before you can qualify for a home loan. We'll discuss credit scores in more detail in the next two sections.

Rent and Your Credit Score

Ironically, most credit scores don't measure the one thing that is perhaps the best predictor of whether someone will pay their mortgage each month: their history of on-time rent payments. Some newer credit score models now incorporate rent payments—if you ask your property manager or landlord to offer electronic payment options that report rent activity to the credit bureaus. But the older FICO scores that mortgage lenders use typically do not. One way to get credit-report cred for your rent payments is to pay your rent by credit card each month, and immediately pay off the card.

Debt-to-Income Ratio (DTI)

Studies have shown that homeowners overwhelmed with too much debt are more likely to default on their mortgages, so lenders also look at something called your debt-to-income ratio. This is the sum of your monthly debts as a percentage of your income.

For example, a couple with $10,000 in monthly income and $3,000 in debt obligations—including the mortgage they're applying for, plus car payments, credit card bills, and the like—has a debt-to-income ratio of 30 percent. Most lenders want your total monthly debts to comprise no more than 43 percent of your income. We'll discuss this in greater detail later in this chapter.

Cash Reserves

As if it's not hard enough to scrounge up a down payment and thousands of dollars in closing costs, lenders often want you to have even *more* cash on hand—enough to cover one or two months of mortgage payments. Thankfully, these cash reserves don't need to be in your checking or savings account; they can be in the form of a 401(k) balance or other assets, like a paid-off car.

Why? Lenders like knowing that, if you lost your job or fell ill, you could still pay your mortgage for a few months if you tapped your emergency fund or cashed out your retirement plan. This isn't as crucial to your application as having enough income or a solid credit history, but it is often a consideration.

Two Years of Steady Employment

Most mortgage lenders want to see a steady, continuous income stream—ideally from the same employer for the past two years. If you haven't worked at your present job for two full years, they'll want to see proof of your previous employment and income, whether through tax returns or old pay stubs.

If you're self-employed, lenders will approach your employment history with extra scrutiny. You'll need two years of tax returns as well as detailed and current profit-and-loss statements to prove your income. We'll discuss this in the Chapter 4 section "What You'll Need to Apply for a Mortgage."

WHY YOUR CREDIT SCORE MATTERS, AND HOW TO FIND YOURS

The Elusive Three-Digit Number That Can Impact Your Life

As confusing, mysterious, and sometimes even unfair as credit scores can be, lenders and other decision makers rely on them to get a quick snapshot of a borrower's fiscal responsibility. That means a good credit score opens doors of opportunity.

Home buyers with very good or excellent credit—a score in the mid-700s or better—can generally qualify for lower interest rates on a mortgage, allowing them to afford a higher-priced home without a higher monthly payment. Of course, it's also easier to obtain a low-interest car loan or open up a new credit card with a good credit score, but those are hardly the only perks of good credit.

Cell phone providers may check your credit score before offering you a two-year payment plan on a new iPhone, for instance, and insurance companies sometimes charge higher premiums to customers with poor credit. In some states, employers and landlords can even check your credit score to determine whether or not to hire or rent to you.

And yet this three-digit number with so much sway over your financial life can be slippery and hard to pin down. There are two main reasons for that. First, we all have *many different credit scores*, created by competing companies for various purposes. Second, credit scores are proprietary information, meaning the companies that produce them control and carefully guard the algorithms used to create their scores.

FICO VERSUS VANTAGESCORE

The two main credit scoring models are FICO and VantageScore. FICO is named for the Fair Isaac Corporation, which pioneered credit scoring decades ago; it remains the most commonly used score among mortgage lenders. VantageScore is a newer competitor owned by the three major credit reporting agencies: Experian, Equifax, and TransUnion. (These companies each keep track of your credit history, and all credit scores are based on the information they have on file. We'll look at the credit reporting agencies in greater detail in a bit.)

So right off the bat, you have at least two credit scores, both of which can change daily based on your most recent financial behavior. Both of these scoring models also have various iterations in use—sort of like computer operating systems. Some industries, or specific lenders, may use older versions of either FICO or VantageScore, whether due to compatibility issues or comfort level. Most mortgage lenders still use classic versions of the FICO score, according to Experian.

What's more, scores can be customized for different clients—an automobile lender, for example, may be more concerned with someone's history of repaying car loans than whether they were late making a credit card payment. FICO alone uses dozens of different credit scoring models, according to the Consumer Financial Protection Bureau.

HOW TO FIND YOUR CREDIT SCORE

How do you learn what your credit score is in this dizzying sea of numbers? The good news is, recent legislation has made it easier for consumers to access their credit scores without cost. While you have many different credit scores, they're all based on the same information—the data found in one or more of your three credit reports. Therefore, if you learn one score, you'll have a pretty good sense of where your other scores should be as well.

For most consumers, the simplest way to find your credit score is now through your credit card. Most card issuers, including American Express, Capital One, Chase, and Discover, offer a free look at either your FICO or VantageScore credit score—just poke around the online dashboard when you log in to pay your credit card bill.

If your card issuer doesn't offer this perk (or if you don't have a credit card), the banks just mentioned offer this service to anyone who sets up a free account online, not just cardholders.

You can also purchase your FICO score from www.myfico.com for a one-time fee of $20 to $60. (You don't need to pay for credit monitoring or other ongoing subscriptions.) The lower price gets you a FICO score based on one of your three credit reports; the full price provides a more complete score based on all three of your credit profiles.

Yes, that's right: Even the same credit scoring model can produce three different credit scores, depending on which of your three credit reports it's based on.

All three credit reporting agencies should theoretically have the same information about you—so most consumers find that their scores are pretty consistent across the board. But if one of the reporting agencies has an error on your file, your scores may differ, sometimes dramatically.

And mistakes happen all the time, especially if you have a common name, share an address with lots of people (as in a big or high-turnover apartment building), or sometimes go by a nickname. It's crucial to check all three of your credit reports once a year and review them for errors. We'll discuss how to do that, and other ways to improve your credit score, in the next section.

HOW TO IMPROVE YOUR CREDIT SCORE

Tried-and-True (and Legal) Ways to Build or Boost Your Credit

Okay, you've got one of your credit scores for reference—now what?

Well, first it helps to know where you stand. Most consumer credit scores fall on a scale of 300–850. Scores above 800 are considered excellent, but anything above 740 will generally allow you to qualify for the best mortgage interest rates and loan terms. Borrowers with good or fair credit can still get a mortgage, but they may need to pay higher interest rates or use an FHA loan, since conventional lenders will view them as higher risk.

Here's how FICO breaks down its credit score ranges:

- **Poor:** 579 or less
- **Fair:** 580–669
- **Good:** 670–739
- **Very good:** 740–799
- **Excellent:** 800+

If your credit score isn't in "very good" territory, it can be well worth the time and effort to get it there. Boosting your credit score, even by 20 or 40 points, can get you a lower mortgage rate—saving you tens of thousands of dollars in interest over the life of the loan. If your credit score is in the 500s, improving it may be the difference between qualifying for a mortgage and being shut out entirely.

Here are some steps to improve your credit score and tips for building a good score if you don't have much of a credit history yet.

Check Your Credit Reports for Errors

Remember, your credit score is based on the information in your credit reports, so make sure those reports are accurate. You're legally entitled to one free copy of your credit report each year from each of the three credit reporting agencies (Experian, Equifax, and TransUnion). You can request your free copy online at AnnualCreditReport.com or by calling 877-322-8228; you'll need to provide your name, date of birth, Social Security number, and address.

Whether you request all three at once or stagger them throughout the year, review the information in each report and look for any mistakes such as unfamiliar accounts or incorrect addresses or phone numbers.

If you spot any errors, dispute them with the credit reporting agency immediately, in writing and by certified mail. This is free to do, and the agency is generally required to resolve the matter in thirty days. You should also contact in writing the company that supplied the incorrect information in the first place—for example, a bank or credit card company—to update their records.

Correcting an erroneous negative item on your credit report is one of the fastest ways to improve your credit score, perhaps dramatically.

Pay Down Credit Card Balances

Another way to immediately boost your credit score is to pay down your credit card balances. Thirty percent of your credit score is based on something called your credit utilization rate—this is the amount of your available credit you've used up.

For example, if your credit card has a $10,000 limit, and you have a $4,000 balance when a lender runs your credit score—even if you pay off the card in full later that month—your credit utilization rate would be 40 percent at the time the score is created. Experts say that a rate over 30 percent starts to hurt your credit score, and a utilization rate of 10 percent or less is ideal.

So in general it's good practice not to max out your credit cards. But for an immediate credit score boost, pay down your credit card balances. Some personal finance experts even pay off their credit cards twice a month to avoid tiptoeing over that 30 percent threshold.

Ask for a Higher Credit Limit

There's another side to that equation, of course: You can also lower your utilization rate by increasing your available credit line. While a $2,000 balance on a credit card with a $5,000 limit amounts to an unfavorable 40 percent utilization rate, the same balance against a $10,000 limit would drop that rate to 20 percent.

If you've had your credit card for a while and have kept up with payments, it's worth calling your card issuer and asking if they can increase your credit limit (without performing a "hard inquiry" on your credit file, which can temporarily lower your score).

Hard versus Soft Credit Inquiries

When you apply for new credit—whether it's a Home Depot card or a home loan—the lender runs a credit check, resulting in a "hard inquiry" on your credit profile. Any such inquiries used to make lending decisions can cause a minor, temporary drop in your credit score. (This is why experts suggest shopping for a mortgage within a forty-five-day period: All credit checks conducted in that time frame will count as a single hard inquiry.) A "soft inquiry," however, has no effect on your credit score. So when an insurance company looks at your credit profile, for example, or if you check your score online, that's considered a soft inquiry, and it won't impact your credit score.

Have Someone Add You As an Authorized User

One more quick (and legal—be careful with services you see online promising fast credit repair) strategy to improve your credit score is to have a family member with a good and lengthy credit history add you as an authorized user to one of their credit cards. Doing so increases your available credit (helping your utilization rate) and can increase the length of your credit history (which accounts for another 15 percent of your credit score).

This comes with inherent risks: Family and money can be a tricky combination, and each of you can now influence the other's credit profile. But if done thoughtfully—say, adding your name to a card a family member has had for many years but rarely uses anymore, and cutting up the extra card so you don't use it either—this can give a relatively quick lift to your credit score.

Don't Close Old Accounts

Got an old credit card that you never use anymore? Great. Cut it up, or put it in a drawer and forget about it, but *don't close the account.* Since 15 percent of your credit score is based on the length of your credit history, that old credit card is quietly doing hero's work on your behalf. (If it's charging you a pesky annual fee, ask the card issuer to migrate your account to a no-fee card.)

Pay On Time, Every Time, Over Time

Consistently on-time payments are the bread and butter of a good credit score. A single on-time payment won't provide an instantaneous boost. But because payment history accounts for 35 percent of your credit score, every month that you make full and on-time payments toward your debts will incrementally improve your score.

Meanwhile, just one late payment (more than thirty days past due) can cause your score to drop suddenly. While its negative impact will fade over time, that delinquency will linger on your credit report for seven years.

Set up text alerts, phone reminders, autopay plans, or anything else you need to ensure that you never miss a payment on your car loan, credit cards (including store cards), student loans, or other bills. If you're worried about overdrawing from your checking account, most credit cards allow you to set up autopay for just the minimum payment, which could be as low as $25; that will ensure you don't miss a payment by accident, though you'll want to pay down your entire balance each month if possible.

It's an unglamorous slog, but paying your bills on time and in full, month after month, year after year, is the very best way to build and maintain a good credit profile. Buying a home takes time, so get started now—and by the time your lender is ready to run your credit, you may already see some improvement.

WHAT IS YOUR DEBT-TO-INCOME RATIO?

(And Why Does It Matter?)

Your credit score isn't the only snapshot number used to gauge your mortgage readiness. Lenders don't want you to carry more debt than you can handle, so they look at your debt-to-income ratio, or DTI. This is the sum of all your monthly debt obligations divided by your monthly gross income; it's sometimes referred to as your back-end DTI.

To calculate your debt-to-income ratio, lenders tally up the total of your mandatory, recurring debts. That includes car payments, student loans, personal loans, alimony or child support payments, and minimum credit card payments, as well as expected housing costs: your potential mortgage, property taxes, home insurance, and any required HOA fees. Nondebt payments, even if they're required (such as health insurance or utility bills), are not included. Then they divide that total by your gross (pretax) monthly income, to see what portion of your earnings is already spoken for each month.

How to Calculate Your Debt-to-Income Ratio

Here's the formula for calculating your DTI: Take the total of all your monthly debts and divide that number by your monthly pretax income. Then multiply the result by 100 to get a percentage:

(Total monthly debts ÷ Gross monthly income) × 100 = DTI ratio

Let's walk through an example. Say you earn $60,000 a year before taxes. To find your gross monthly income, you'd divide that by 12 months: $60,000 ÷ 12 = $5,000. If your monthly debts include a $400 car payment and $100 in student loans, and you're applying for a mortgage with a $2,000 monthly payment (including estimated taxes and insurance), that would bring your total debt burden to $2,500 a month. Dividing $2,500 in debts by $5,000 in monthly income would give you a debt-to-income ratio of 50 percent:

$$\$2,500 ÷ \$5,000 = 0.50 × 100 = 50 \text{ percent}$$

That's probably not going to cut it. Most lenders require that your total debt-to-income ratio be no more than 43 percent or 45 percent. (There are exceptions, however. In 2019, more than a quarter of FHA loans went to borrowers with a DTI ratio over 50 percent. And Fannie Mae now allows a DTI of up to 50 percent in limited cases, with some very big caveats: Applicants must have excellent credit, at least a 20 percent down payment, and twelve months' worth of cash reserves.)

Getting under that 43 percent threshold would require one of two things: adding more income to the mix or removing some of the debt.

If you got a big raise and now earn $6,000 a month, for example, that same $2,500 in debt would represent a 42 percent DTI ratio—still high, but just under the limit.

Alternatively, if your income remained unchanged, but you sold your car or waited until you paid it off to apply for the mortgage, that would reduce your monthly debt burden to $2,100 in total, and your new DTI ratio would be 42 percent.

Of course, another way to lower your debt-to-income ratio (while keeping your car) would be to apply for a smaller mortgage. A $1,600 monthly payment would keep you under the 42 percent limit, even with your car loan and student loan payments.

It's important to note that 43 percent is considered a maximum threshold, not a target. A more comfortable debt-to-income ratio—and one that many stricter lenders even require—is to limit your debts to 36 percent or less of your gross monthly income. By that standard, someone earning $5,000 a month should owe no more than $1,800 of that income in monthly debts, including their mortgage.

Remember the 28 percent rule from the beginning of this chapter? That's a type of debt-to-income ratio as well—what lenders call a front-end DTI, which only looks at housing costs. Some lenders consider both debt-to-income ratios when underwriting a mortgage. Using the front-end DTI ratio, someone earning $5,000 a month shouldn't take on a mortgage payment of more than $1,400 a month—though, again, some lenders will make exceptions. FHA loans allow for a 31 percent front-end DTI ratio, for example, according to *Bankrate*.

If your credit card balances and other debts are standing in the way of getting the mortgage you want, read on. In the next section, we'll look at some strategies for paying down debt.

HOW TO TACKLE YOUR DEBT

Or At Least Get It under Control

Paying down debt—especially high-interest credit card balances—is almost always a smart financial move. However, that "almost" is especially important to note when you're preparing to buy a home. You need to be saving up at least some cash for a down payment and closing costs, a goal that can sometimes be at odds with aggressively paying off debt.

In fact, a lot of the down payment savings strategies we outlined in Chapter 2 can also be used to pay down debt: Any extra money you're able to earn or cut from your budget can be saved—or it could be put toward your unwieldy balances. You'll have to weigh how much of it you want to set aside for your down payment and how much you're comfortable putting toward your debt.

But let's say you've got a modest stash of cash set aside for your down payment, and now you need to focus on lowering your debt-to-income ratio (or just stabilizing your financial situation). Here are some tried-and-true strategies for paying down debt.

Stop Digging Yourself Deeper Into Debt

The first step, always, is to stop putting more charges on your credit cards that you can't pay off right away. If you keep adding to your balances and incurring new interest charges, trying to pay them off will feel like walking up a down escalator.

Pay Off High-Interest Credit Cards First

The average interest rate on a credit card was over 16 percent in May 2021, according to CreditCards.com. That means carrying a

$2,000 balance for a year could cost you $320 in interest; that's money that could be going into your down payment fund but is piling on top of your debt instead. Once you're not paying as much in interest each month, you'll be able to save toward your goal even faster.

Transfer High-Interest Balances

If you have decent credit, you may be able to apply for a balance transfer credit card. These cards allow you to move a high-interest balance from an existing credit card to a new one at a low, promotional interest rate—sometimes 0 percent APR—for a set period, such as twelve or fifteen months. You'll generally have to pay a modest fee, such as $75 or 3 percent of the balance.

This isn't a cure for your debt, but it will buy you time to pay down your balance without fighting an uphill battle against double-digit interest rates. That can help you make faster progress.

What Does APR Mean?

You'll see the acronym APR tossed around in almost every lending scenario, from credit cards to car loans to mortgages. It stands for *annual percentage rate*, which shows the cost of borrowing a sum of money, including fees, as a percent of the loan. A loan's APR will generally be slightly higher than its regular interest rate, because the APR includes any fees you may have to pay. But that helps in making apples-to-apples comparisons of different loans.

Try the "Debt Snowball" Method

Like building credit, paying down debt takes time. But once you get on a roll, you might surprise yourself with how much progress you can make. The "debt snowball" method allows you to start small and log some early victories to build and maintain your debt-busting momentum.

Here's how it works: Say you have three credit cards, with balances of $900 (Card A), $1,700 (Card B), and $4,800 (Card C). And let's say you're able to put an extra $300 a month toward your debt. You'll start by putting it all toward the smallest balance, Card A, while making only the minimum payments (say, $50 a month) on the other two cards.

After three months, Card A is paid off—good job! Now, add the $300 you had been paying toward it to the $50 you've been paying on Card B. That's the snowball effect—your outlay hasn't changed, but you're now making a bigger dent. At $350 a month, you'll have Card B paid off in five months. Then, you can add that $350 to the $50 a month you've been paying on Card C, which you'll have knocked out in a year at what is now a $400-a-month pace.

WHAT ABOUT OTHER DEBTS?

Some debts—installment loans, they're called, because they're paid as fixed monthly sums—are often considered "good debt." Student loans, mortgages, and auto loans generally have low interest rates and help, rather than hurt, your credit score (so long as you pay them on time).

However, if your debt-to-income ratio is too high to qualify for the mortgage you want, and it's due to a car or student loan, you might want to explore some of these options:

- **Apply for an income-based repayment plan:** If you have a federal student loan, look into an income-driven repayment plan that will cap what you owe each month at 10 percent or 20 percent of your discretionary income.

- **Refinance private student loans:** You generally *never* want to refinance federal student loans, because you'll forfeit future benefits (such as the potential for loan forgiveness). But refinancing private loans can lower your monthly payments by stretching the balance out over a longer term; however, unless you can score a lower interest rate, you'll typically pay a lot more interest over the life of the loan.

- **Trade in, sell, or pay off your car:** If your car payment is tipping your debt-to-income ratio over the edge, consider whether you could trade it in for a less expensive model or sell it and get by with a cheap used car (or no car at all) for a little while. Or, if you've only got a few more months of payments due, pay it off early so it's no longer counted toward your monthly debt obligations.

Chapter 4

Understanding Mortgages

A mortgage is just another loan, like you'd use to buy a car. So why does it feel so daunting?

For one thing, the stakes are much higher. Instead of a five-year auto loan, this one may last thirty years—more than a generation. It takes weeks and mountains of paperwork to secure one and includes strange terminology like *points*. You're pledging to pay hundreds of thousands of dollars, and tens of thousands more in total interest charges. And if you don't pay it, you could literally be kicked out of your own home. So, yeah...a mortgage can seem a little scary.

Yet it's also something of a miracle. The thirty-year, fixed-rate mortgage didn't even exist a hundred years ago—and still doesn't, in many other countries. The ability to finance a home purchase through a predictable, long-term payment plan has opened up homeownership to millions of Americans who could never afford it otherwise.

In this chapter, you'll come to understand the mortgage process. You'll learn the ins and outs of home loans, from how they work to how to compare them, and why they're not to be feared.

HOW DO MORTGAGES WORK?

The Mechanics of a Home Loan

If you're a first-time buyer, it's very likely that you'll need a loan to purchase a home—not many folks have a few hundred thousand dollars just kicking around somewhere. Home buying loans, which are offered through banks, credit unions, and other lenders, are called mortgages. Here's how they work.

When you take out a mortgage, you literally promise (in what is called a promissory note) to repay the money, in monthly installments, according to a defined set of terms. These terms include the length of the loan (e.g., fifteen or thirty years) and the interest rate, among other details. Until you pay off the entire mortgage, you and the bank are essentially partners, or co-owners.

The amount you borrow is called the principal. For the privilege of borrowing all that money upfront, you'll also pay your lender interest on the loan. Since it's a big loan, spread out over many years, even a small change in your interest rate can have a profound effect on how much you'll pay over the life of the mortgage.

Like a car loan, a mortgage is a secured loan, meaning the lender holds an asset as collateral. In the case of an auto loan, a lender can repossess your car if you stop making payments; with a mortgage, your home itself is the collateral. That removes some of the risk for the lender and in turn allows them to loan you money at a lower interest rate. (A credit card is an example of an unsecured loan. The card issuer lends you money to buy stuff without holding anything as collateral, which is one reason credit card interest rates are much higher than mortgage rates.)

You might hear a lender mention LTV, which is your loan-to-value ratio. This is really just a different way of expressing your down payment. If you're putting down 5 percent of the purchase price, the lender is loaning you 95 percent of the home's value, meaning your LTV is 95 percent. A high LTV loan is riskier for a lender, so a mortgage with an LTV above 80 percent will generally require private mortgage insurance.

Finally, many lenders may require you to pay into an escrow account, from which your local property taxes and home insurance bills are paid. Basically, this just means that your monthly mortgage payment consists of not just principal and interest but also taxes and insurance. Lenders use the acronym PITI to refer to this bundle: principal, interest, taxes, and insurance.

FIXED-RATE VERSUS ADJUSTABLE-RATE MORTGAGES

Mortgages come in all varieties, but perhaps the most important distinction to understand is that between fixed- and adjustable-rate mortgages.

Fixed-Rate Mortgages

The vast majority of borrowers use a thirty-year, fixed-rate mortgage to purchase their home, especially when interest rates are low. No matter the length of the loan term, a fixed-rate mortgage just means that your interest rate won't change, and your combined principal and interest payment will stay the same for the entire loan term. (Property taxes and insurance can still go up, though.)

While your monthly payment stays the same, the way it's split up between principal and interest changes over time; this is called your amortization schedule. In the early years of a thirty-year mortgage, most of your monthly payment goes toward interest. As time goes on, more and more of your payment is directed toward the principal each month, helping you gain more equity in your home.

However, as long as your mortgage doesn't have a prepayment penalty—that's when lenders charge a fee for paying off a loan early, a practice that's been outlawed in some states—you can put extra money toward your principal balance at any time to pay off your mortgage faster.

"Investing" in Your Mortgage

Rounding up your mortgage payment each month—when you can afford to—can help you build equity faster and pay off your loan years sooner. For example, say you take out a thirty-year mortgage for $300,000 at a fixed 4 percent rate. Your monthly payment, before taxes and insurance, would be $1,432.25; over thirty years, you'd pay about $215,600 in total interest.

If you simply rounded up that cumbersome payment to an even $1,500 each month, thereby paying an extra $67.75 toward your loan principal, you would own your home outright two and a half years sooner and pay $25,400 less in total interest. As long as your loan doesn't have a prepayment penalty, the only downside to this strategy is having $67.75 less to spend or save for retirement each month. But by paying down the mortgage debt, you're essentially "investing" at a guaranteed 4 percent rate of return.

Adjustable-Rate Mortgages (ARMs)

When mortgage rates are high, some home buyers take a gamble on adjustable-rate loans. These offer lower introductory interest rates for a fixed amount of time, after which the rate can change annually.

ARMs are often expressed in numerical shorthand, such as $5/1$ or $7/1$, where the first number is the fixed, introductory period, and the second number is how often the rate can change afterward (in years). For example, a $5/1$ ARM at 3.0 percent means that your interest rate will be fixed at 3.0 percent for the first five years, after which it will readjust once a year to the going market rate—which could be just as low, but could also be much higher. These loans have fallen out of fashion in recent years but can sometimes make sense for buyers who intend to resell in just a few years.

Refinancing

Here's something to keep in the back of your mind: You don't need to keep the same mortgage forever. Refinancing is when you replace your current loan with a new one—ideally one with better terms. It's fairly expensive to do, because you'll pay closing costs all over again. But if interest rates drop or your credit improves significantly, refinancing your mortgage can end up saving you money or lowering your monthly payment.

At the same time, there's no guarantee that you'll be able to refinance precisely when you want to. If your income has dropped, or if home values have fallen, it may be hard to qualify for a new mortgage. So it's worth trying to get the best mortgage you can the first time around.

PREAPPROVAL VERSUS PREQUALIFICATION

One Carries More Weight Than the Other

When you start poking around on mortgage lender websites, you'll see links beckoning you to "Get prequalified!" Prequalification is a good and useful exercise, but it's generally not the same—not by a long shot—as getting preapproved.

WHAT IS PREQUALIFICATION?

In most cases, getting prequalified starts with entering your financial information, to the best of your knowledge, on a lender's website. Their algorithms can then automatically and quickly tell you, based on the information you've provided, what kind of mortgage you can expect to qualify for—assuming that everything you entered is accurate.

That's extremely useful information for you to have (and it's generally free to get), so you should give it a try. Some lenders might ask for permission to pull your credit score, to offer a more precise assessment, and you may even receive a letter of prequalification. However, that doesn't really mean much to anyone else, because it's all based on your own self-attested estimates.

Consider this type of prequalification an educational first step as you dip your toes into the mortgage pool.

Proof Matters

So-called no-doc loans—mortgages lenders issued based solely on a buyer's stated income (with no documentation required)—were a risky but prevalent practice during the run-up to the housing crash of the mid- to late-2000s. Spoiler alert: It didn't work out well for anybody.

WHAT IS PREAPPROVAL?

Getting preapproved for a mortgage is more like taking the plunge, or at least wading in waist-deep. Instead of just typing in your income and down payment savings on a web form, you'll upload (or provide hard copies of) documents such as your pay stubs, tax returns, and bank statements.

A loan officer will then verify all the information and run a check on your credit score too. If everything looks good, you'll receive a preapproval letter that's valid for a specified amount of time, such as thirty or ninety days. You'll include a copy of this letter with any offer you make to purchase a home.

It's the Docs That Count

Some lenders may call this preapproval stage verified prequalification or some other term. Whatever the name, the important point is that you've provided documented evidence to support your loan application.

The preapproval process is usually free, but because it involves some real work on the part of the lender, you may have to pay an application fee. That money could be credited back to you at closing if you ultimately end up using the same lender for your mortgage. But at this stage, you're under no obligation to actually take out a mortgage with that lender, and their offer to you is only preliminary.

A preapproval letter carries real weight when you make an offer on a home, though. It means a lender has reviewed and accepted evidence of your income, down payment funds, and credit history, and is fully prepared to lend you that amount of money, provided a few final conditions are met.

For example, the exact amount you're preapproved for could change if interest rates rise, throwing the math off a bit. As well, once you're ready to purchase a specific home, your lender will require an independent appraiser to assess the home's value—to make sure it's worth at least as much as they're lending you. Still, a preapproval letter demonstrates that a bank believes in you, so sellers will take your offer much more seriously.

WHAT IS PRE-UNDERWRITING, OR UNDERWRITTEN PREAPPROVAL?

Loan officers are the front-line, customer-facing employees at a mortgage lender, but underwriters are the number crunchers who ultimately give any loan the final stamp of approval. Other times, though, they're the behind-the-scenes forces who squash home buying dreams two weeks before closing, because the numbers don't quite add up the way the loan officer thought they did. Bottom line: In the end your home loan all comes down to underwriting.

In a competitive housing market, some Realtors suggest getting underwritten preapproval—meaning your application has already gone through the full underwriting process. That means your offer is almost as good as cash in the eyes of a seller, because there's very little chance that your financing is going to fall through a few days before closing.

If your application is a fairly straightforward one, some lenders may offer automatic underwriting free of charge. But generally, taking this step will start to trigger application fees, and more or less lock you in to working with that particular lender—so make sure you're happy with your mortgage lender first. That said, it's a very useful strategy in a hot housing market.

WHAT YOU'LL NEED TO APPLY FOR A MORTGAGE

Get Ready for Some Serious Paperwork

Ready to apply for a mortgage? Here are the documents and information that you (and your co-borrower, if you're applying with a spouse or partner) will need to round up. Most lenders now allow you to upload PDFs online or to grant them temporary access to your financial accounts, but you can also gather the documents the old-fashioned way and submit hard copies in person.

Personal Information

You'll need to provide an official form of identification, such as your driver's license, plus all the usual identifying information, including your name, address, date of birth, and Social Security number.

Proof of Income

If you're a salaried employee, you'll need to supply at least two recent pay stubs plus your employer's contact info (lenders may call your company's human resources or payroll department to verify your income and length of employment). Your lender may also want to see your last two W-2 forms and the last two years of your tax returns.

If there are gaps in your employment or income within the past two years, you may have to write a formal letter explaining the circumstances of those interruptions and why they shouldn't diminish your long-term earnings or employment prospects.

Self-employed borrowers and small business owners will definitely need to provide two or more years of tax returns along with a signed copy of IRS Form 4506-T, which authorizes a lender to verify your tax returns against IRS records. You'll also need to submit detailed profit-and-loss statements from the past two years. That may sound daunting if you're not terribly organized, but you essentially just need to itemize your business revenue and expenses on a monthly or quarterly basis up to the present day. You can find and download free profit-and-loss templates online to get you started. Enter your total gross earnings or sales revenue for each month, and then itemize your expenses—such as utilities, supplies, marketing fees, mileage and tolls, health insurance, employee wages, and the like. Subtract your expenses from your total earnings to find your net profit (or loss); that's the figure a lender is going to use as your monthly pretax income.

To Deduct or Not to Deduct?

As a small business owner or sole proprietor, you're probably accustomed to writing off as many tax-deductible business expenses as you legally can to reduce your taxable income each year. However, that could come back to haunt you when it's time to apply for a mortgage, since it may appear—to a lender, at least—that you're not earning enough to afford a home. If you know you're going to be house hunting next year, you might want to ask a financial advisor whether it's worth being a little less aggressive with your tax deductions this year.

Bank Statements

Lenders also want to see proof of your down payment funds, so you'll need to list your assets and hand over statements from your checking and savings accounts. (Aggravatingly, even though you're supplying the lender with official bank statements that show this information, you may also be asked to fill out a form with all of your account numbers and balances too.) If there are any large, unusual deposits from the past sixty days, such as a gift from a family member, your lender will probably ask for a letter of explanation. (See the section on using financial gifts for a down payment in Chapter 2.)

Retirement Account Statements

If you have a 401(k), 403(b), IRA, or other type of investment account, print out your most recent statement(s). Even if you have no intention of cashing out these accounts, such assets will strengthen your loan application in the eyes of a lender.

Credit Card and Loan Statements

Remember, one of the things lenders are most concerned with is your debt-to-income ratio. So you'll need to submit the most recent statements for any credit cards, student loans, car loans, and other debts you carry. Once again, you may have to fill out every sixteen-digit account number on an official form, despite providing printed statements with the same information.

Rent Checks and Landlord References

If you currently rent your home, you may be asked to demonstrate a history of paying rent on time by showing canceled rent checks and providing your landlord's contact information as a reference. If your credit is at all iffy, you can definitely expect this step.

Other Documents

Depending on your situation, your lender may request a variety of other supporting documentation to strengthen your application.

For example, if your income includes alimony or child support, you may need to provide copies of court records or cashed checks that prove that recent payments were made. Or if your credit history is thin, some lenders may only be willing to work with you if you can provide plenty of proof of on-time rent and utility payments. Be ready to supply whatever information your lender requests—within reason—in a prompt manner to keep your application on track.

What Lenders Can't Ask

While a mortgage lender can and will ask for all kinds of financial information, a couple of topics are off-limits. They are not permitted to ask you whether you plan to have children (or more of them), and they're not allowed to inquire about health issues or disabilities.

HOW RATES IMPACT YOUR PURCHASING POWER

And the Ultimate Price of Your Home

There are a lot of moving parts to a mortgage, and we've covered the ones that are somewhat within your command—your income, credit score, savings, and debt. But one key variable is largely beyond your control: interest rates.

Each lender ultimately sets its own interest rates on various loan products, but rates tend to fluctuate based on the broader financial markets.

The Federal Reserve and Mortgage Rates

There's a widespread misconception that the Federal Reserve determines mortgage rates, but the relationship is not nearly that simple. The Fed sets a target for the federal funds rate, which is the rate banks pay to the US Treasury to borrow money. That, in turn, influences but does not control the prime rate, which banks charge customers, and other rates all over the world, from the price of a ten-year Treasury bond to the rates consumers see on mortgages. Sometimes, however, rates rise or drop despite the Fed's actions, simply based on investor sentiment.

While there's no way to predict the market-based movements of interest rates, you'll still want to pay close attention to mortgage rates as you begin house hunting. Because even minor swings can dramatically change which homes fit into your price range.

An increase of just half a percentage point on a thirty-year mortgage rate—from 2.75 percent to 3.25 percent, for example—can decrease a home buyer's purchasing power by more than $23,000, according to a study by Redfin, even if nothing else about their financial situation has changed.

On the other hand, just a small drop in mortgage rates can suddenly put a more expensive home within reach. A couple preapproved for a $2,000 monthly payment at 4 percent, for instance, could take out a $419,000 loan. If their interest rate dropped to 3.5 percent, they could suddenly borrow up to $445,000 without increasing their monthly payment, adding $26,000 to their purchasing power.

Record-low interest rates were one reason home prices skyrocketed all across the United States in 2020, despite a deadly pandemic and a sharp recession. The sudden economic slowdown made investors more cautious, which, along with support from the Federal Reserve and a drop in the federal funds rate, pulled interest rates lower on everything from mortgages to savings bonds. And with the average interest rate on a thirty-year mortgage falling below 3 percent for much of the year, according to Freddie Mac's Primary Mortgage Market Survey, home buyers suddenly had more room in their budgets, which they used to bid home prices up even higher.

LONG-TERM IMPACT

Your interest rate doesn't just impact your monthly mortgage payment and how much home you can afford; it also determines how much you'll pay for your home in the long run.

Let's say you take out a thirty-year, $250,000 mortgage to pay for a $300,000 home. At a 4 percent interest rate, you'll pay a total of

$179,674 in interest if you keep the loan and the home for all thirty years—bringing the final price tag of your home to $479,674.

That's a pretty hefty premium. But at a 4.5 percent interest rate—just half a percentage point more—you'd pay a total of $206,017 in interest over thirty years, an extra $26,343 that brings the ultimate cost of your home to $506,017.

Granted, this is not as bad a deal as it sounds: You're getting a home to live in *now* in exchange for what are largely future, inflated dollars. Most consumer goods tend to rise in price over time, an economic concept known as inflation. Consider that the price of everything from a postage stamp to a loaf of bread to a movie ticket has roughly doubled in price over the past thirty years—to say nothing of housing, daycare, college tuition, or even admission to Disney World. That's inflation in action. So it's quite possible that a $1,200 mortgage payment will, in twenty-five to thirty years, feel more like the equivalent of a $600 payment in today's money. But the point is, even a small change in your interest rate can make a big difference.

Now, even though rates fluctuate with market conditions, your loan's interest rate isn't *totally* beyond your control. You can and should shop around for the best combination of low rates and low fees that you can find, for example. But there is one more way to lower your interest rate, no matter whom you borrow from—and that's by purchasing "points," which we'll explain next.

WHAT ARE POINTS?

And What's the Point of Them?

You may see lower-than-normal mortgage rates advertised with something called points. Mortgage points, sometimes called discount points, essentially amount to prepaid interest: Lenders allow you to buy down the interest rate on your mortgage by paying a fee upfront. That means you're paying more money now to save some money in the long run.

One point generally costs 1 percent of the loan—i.e., $1,000 per $100,000 borrowed. And while the exact discount on the rate can vary, each point purchased normally lowers the long-term mortgage rate by roughly a quarter of a percentage point (reducing the rate from 4.5 percent to 4.25 percent, for instance) for the life of the loan.

For example, say you're looking to take out a thirty-year, fixed-rate mortgage of $300,000 at a rate of 3.5 percent. Before taxes and insurance, your mortgage payment would be about $1,347 a month, and you'd end up paying about $185,000 in total interest over thirty years.

If you purchased one point to lower your interest rate, you'd pay an extra $3,000 upfront (ouch). But with a lower rate of 3.25 percent, your monthly payment would drop by $42 to $1,305, and you'd pay about $170,000 in total interest—saving nearly $12,000 total in the long term, after accounting for the upfront payment.

Whether it makes sense to buy mortgage points boils down to two questions:

1. Do you even have enough cash on hand to pay for points on top of your down payment and closing costs? For many first-time buyers, any extra cash would be better directed toward a bigger

down payment or a remodeling fund, so this makes buying points moot.

2. If you do have the cash, how long do you intend to stay in the home before selling it or refinancing? Purchasing points to lower your interest rate only makes sense if you keep the mortgage long enough to break even on the upfront expense. You can find your break-even date by dividing the cost of the points by the monthly savings. In the previous example, dividing $3,000 by the $42 in monthly savings comes out to 71.4 months. Divide that by 12, and it would take about a full six years just to recoup the upfront costs.

Time Is Money

Remember how we talked about inflation and how the value of a dollar tends to slowly erode over time? That's one more thing to consider before you pay for mortgage points: You're paying present-day money to save less-valuable future money.

POINTS CARRY TAX BENEFITS

Once you become a homeowner, you may want to start itemizing your taxes. This is, frankly, kind of a pain in the neck—but it's often worth the effort, since you're able to deduct any interest paid on a mortgage of up to $750,000, as well as some of your property taxes, from your taxable income.

Because banks front-load interest into the early years of a mortgage, you may end up with quite a bit of interest to deduct in the first years of homeownership. For example, take a thirty-year, $300,000 mortgage with a 4.5 percent interest rate. In the first year, you'll pay $13,400 in mortgage interest, which can be deducted from your taxable income (reducing the amount of income that can be taxed). You can also deduct up to $10,000 in property taxes. Because points are essentially prepaid mortgage interest, you can deduct the full value of any points paid in the year that you paid them.

The tax overhaul passed in 2017 just about doubled the standard deduction—the amount that everybody gets to knock off their taxable income as a starting point—making this process unnecessary for some homeowners. Itemizing used to be almost a no-brainer for homeowners; now, it only makes sense to itemize your tax deductions if they come out to be more than the standard deduction, which in 2021 is $12,550 for single taxpayers and $25,100 for married couples filing jointly. But if you purchased a discount point on that $300,000 mortgage, that's an additional $3,000 in tax deductions—perhaps enough to make itemizing worthwhile, at least in your first year of homeownership.

COMPARE POINTS TO POINTS

As you shop around for mortgages, always ask to see the rate *before* any points are applied, so you can more easily compare different loans. And when you see a surprisingly low advertised rate, pay attention to whether it hinges on borrowers purchasing 1, 2, or even 3 points.

WHAT IS PMI?

All about Private Mortgage Insurance

Another unfamiliar term that might impact your mortgage payment is PMI, which stands for *private mortgage insurance.*

If your down payment is less than 20 percent of the purchase price, most lenders will require you to take out private mortgage insurance. The cost will vary depending on your down payment size and credit score, but PMI averages $30 to $70 a month per $100,000 borrowed, according to Freddie Mac. On a $300,000 mortgage, that's an extra $90 to $210 tacked onto your monthly payment—and lenders will count it against your debt-to-income ratio.

Unfortunately, this added expense isn't even an insurance policy for you—it's to protect the lender, should you default on your loan. (When a borrower makes a down payment of 20 percent or more, the bank has some financial cushion if it ever needs to foreclose on the property, pay back taxes, and resell the home at a loss. But if a bank is financing 95 percent of the purchase price, it faces a greater risk of losing money in the event of a default—hence, PMI.)

GETTING RID OF PMI

The good news is that, in most cases, PMI doesn't last forever. As you pay down your loan principal, and as your home's value appreciates, you'll gradually build equity in your home—that is, the difference between what your home is worth and what you still owe on it. Once your equity stake reaches 20 percent of the home's value—the amount of a traditional down payment—you can ask your lender to cancel the PMI on your loan. Once you hit 22 percent of the home's original sale price, the lender must stop charging you PMI by law, as long as you're current on your payments.

Here are a couple of examples of how that might play out. Say you're buying a home for $300,000, and you have a 5 percent down payment ($15,000). You take out a thirty-year, $285,000 mortgage at 4.5 percent. After a little more than eight years of monthly payments, you'll have paid down the principal to below $240,000, meaning your equity stake has reached the 20 percent threshold. (If you owe $240,000 on a $300,000 home, you have $60,000 in home equity.) At that point, you can request to stop paying PMI, and your lender might oblige—though they may ask you to get a fresh home appraisal. (If they refuse, you could now look into refinancing with another lender, PMI-free.) About a year later, after nine and a half years of mortgage payments, you would hit the 22 percent equity benchmark—which triggers an automatic termination of your PMI payments by law. Suddenly, you'd find yourself with an extra hundred bucks or more a month at your disposal.

However, you can often get rid of PMI much sooner than eight or nine years into a mortgage. Let's say that home values appreciate 5 percent a year in your area. After just three years, your $300,000 home would be worth about $347,000, while your remaining principal would be down to $270,000—giving you more than a 20 percent equity stake in your home. At that point, you could ask your lender to get the PMI off your loan. (Again, they may require a new appraisal.)

Alternatively (or additionally), you could speed up your exit from PMI purgatory by making extra payments toward your principal. Even if your home's value doesn't appreciate one bit, paying an extra $100 toward your principal each month could get your loan balance down to $240,000 a full year and a half sooner.

A Better PMI

While rare, some first-time home buyer programs offer a more consumer-friendly form of mortgage insurance—one that actually protects borrowers *and* lenders. In Massachusetts, for example, MassHousing offers MI Plus, an insurance policy that will pay a borrower's mortgage for up to six months if they lose their job.

PMI by Any Other Name

Private mortgage insurance is used for conventional loans—that is, regular, privately backed mortgages. Loans backed by the government, such as FHA, VA, and USDA loans, don't require private mortgage insurance—except they kind of do. It's just named and handled differently.

On a VA loan, for example, borrowers must pay a one-time VA funding fee, which ranges from 1.4 percent to 3.6 percent of the loan total. This can be paid upfront or wrapped into the loan, but its purpose is largely the same as PMI: to protect the lender (in this case, US taxpayers) against a costly default.

FHA and USDA borrowers, meanwhile, pay both an upfront fee, which can be rolled into the loan, plus an annual fee billed in monthly installments on top of the mortgage. Again, this is essentially PMI by another name.

WHAT ARE CLOSING COSTS?

And Is There Any Way Around Them?

You've likely heard of closing costs by now—but what are they, exactly? Closing costs refer to the many fees associated with buying a home, which are all paid at closing. This assortment of fees varies by location, but you can expect to pay anywhere from 2 percent to 5 percent of the home's sale price in total closing costs, according to *Bankrate*, or nearly $6,000 on average.

Most, but not all, of these fees are related to the mortgage. Even buyers who purchase their home in cash will need to pay some general real estate transaction charges as well. Here are some of the services and fees that, taken collectively, make up closing costs:

- **Appraisal fee:** Before a lender will give you hundreds of thousands of dollars to buy a home, they want to make sure it's a safe investment—that the property is actually worth what they're loaning you. So most will require a third-party appraiser to estimate the home's market value and add the bill (typically a few hundred dollars) to your tab at closing.
- **Title search:** When you take ownership of a home, you could also be taking on any unresolved claims against the property, such as unpaid tax liens or title disputes between a former owner's heirs. For another few hundred bucks, lenders hire a title company to search local property records to make sure the title to your home is "clean"— meaning there are no disputes over the deed or other claims against the property that could complicate the transfer of ownership.
- **Title insurance:** A title search may not turn up every problem, however. So lenders will require you to purchase title insurance,

which protects against any unforeseen issues—for example, if an unpaid contractor files a claim against the property, or if an old typo in the records ends up causing costly confusion. This can cost you anywhere from a couple hundred dollars to over $2,000, but it only protects the lender—an owner's policy costs extra but is recommended.

- **Attorney fees:** Some states require that a real estate lawyer handle the closing process, for which you may have to pick up the tab (or part of it, if the cost is split between buyer and seller). If your purchase is a complicated one, you may want to hire your own attorney as well.

- **Loan origination fees:** In addition to the interest you'll pay over time, lenders usually recoup the cost of preparing, underwriting, and processing your loan by charging an application fee and an underwriting fee. These can amount to 1 percent or more of the loan amount, but they can and will vary—so compare loan estimates from different lenders.

- **Homeowner's insurance and property taxes:** Whether you pay them directly or through an escrow account, your first year of home insurance premiums and your first three to six months of property taxes must be paid at closing.

- **Other miscellaneous fees:** There are many smaller fees in the mix, too, which may range from $20 to $100 or so. For example, you'll need to pay for a notary public to officially notarize your signatures, and the registry of deeds charges a fee to enter the sale into the public record. You may be charged a courier fee to safely transport loan documents. Your lender will probably add the fee for your credit check to the closing costs, and there's a bank fee for processing the loan too.

- **"Stamp" taxes and real estate transfer fees:** Your state, county, city, or homeowners' association—or all of the above—may charge a tax or fee every time a property changes hands. Sometimes these fees are paid by the seller, but in other cases they're split evenly or paid by the buyer.

Transfer Taxes—and Who Pays Them— Will Vary by Location

A difference of just a few miles can cost you a few thousand dollars at closing. In Massachusetts, sellers customarily pay the real estate transfer tax, which amounts to about 0.456 percent of the home price. In neighboring New Hampshire, though, the tax is about three times as much (1.5 percent) and gets split between seller and buyer. Next door in Vermont, the property transfer tax of 1.45 percent and a 0.2 percent clean water surcharge are borne entirely by the buyer. On a $350,000 home, that's an extra $5,775 due at closing.

Meanwhile, in California, counties often layer their own property transfer taxes on top of the statewide rate; in Chicago, sellers pay statewide, county-level, *and* city-level transfer taxes, while buyers are expected to pay a separate city portion that amounts to 0.75 percent of the purchase price. Ask your Realtor what to expect in your area so you're not taken by surprise.

DEALING WITH CLOSING COSTS

That's a lot to keep track of, so always feel free to ask your lender for an explanation if a fee seems excessive or confusing. It's also a lot of money to shell out, especially for a first-time buyer. Here are a few ways you may be able to pay less in closing costs:

- If you qualify for down payment assistance, those funds can typically be applied toward closing costs.
- Lenders may allow you to finance some or all of your closing costs through lender credits, essentially bundling them into your mortgage at a slightly higher interest rate. (This will increase your monthly payment and total interest owed.)
- You can also ask your agent to negotiate seller concessions. In a slow market, a seller may agree to share or cover the closing costs to help a sale go through. More often, though, seller concessions are simply a financial workaround, where you pay a higher price for the house and the seller uses that extra money to pay the closing costs for you.
- Shop around and compare loan estimates from a few lenders—some will be more cost-efficient than others. We'll review how to compare mortgage offers in the next section.

COMPARING LOAN ESTIMATES TO FIND THE BEST MORTGAGE
Everything You Need to Know about a Loan

As you learned earlier in this chapter, it's best to get preapproved for a mortgage before you make an offer on a home. Once you've made an offer—and the seller has accepted it—then it's time to take the next step and officially apply for a mortgage.

Most experts suggest shopping around for a mortgage and applying to three or more different lenders to get the best overall deal. When you do, thanks to legislation passed after the financial crisis, each lender must provide you with a standardized loan estimate that outlines the details of your loan within three business days.

Each three-page loan estimate outlines exactly what your mortgage terms and costs would be were you to buy that specific home using that loan from that particular lender. The numbers are still only estimates, and not set in stone—even if you were preapproved a month ago, the bank may ask for updated pay stubs, for example, and take one last look at your savings—but they're pretty close to final. The standardized format of a loan estimate makes it easy to compare loans side by side to see which one is the best option. (This document used to be called the Good Faith Estimate, and it could vary quite a bit by lender, making comparisons complicated.)

Save the Fees for Closing

A lender shouldn't charge you more than a small credit-check fee—around $20—to get a loan estimate, according to the Consumer Financial Protection Bureau.

WHAT'S IN A LOAN ESTIMATE?

The first page of a loan estimate provides an overview of your potential mortgage. It outlines the type, structure, and amount of the loan, as well as the interest rate, what your monthly payments would be, how much you'd pay in PMI (and for how long), your estimated property taxes and homeowner's insurance, your down payment, and your total closing costs.

The second page breaks down those various closing costs into an itemized list, including which services you can shop around for and which ones you can't. This allows you to compare, say, underwriting fees between different lenders.

You'll also see a breakdown of prepaid expenses, such as your first year of home insurance and property taxes. At the bottom, it tallies up the total amount of cash you'll need to close, including your down payment, any deposits you've already paid, and any lender or seller credits toward your closing costs.

On the third page, you'll find some fine print, but also a helpful "comparisons" section, with three important numbers you can use to compare one loan with another:

- **In Five Years:** This tells you how much money you'll pay on the loan over your first five years and how much principal you'll have paid down in that time. All else being equal, you'd want a lower first number (overall payments) and a higher second number (giving you more equity in the home faster).

- **Annual Percentage Rate (APR):** This isn't your actual mortgage interest rate but rather is a way to compare all the combined costs of a loan. The APR factors in both the interest charges and the various lender fees and expresses that total as a percentage of the loan. When comparing two loan estimates, the lower APR indicates a less expensive loan overall.
- **Total Interest Percentage (TIP):** This may feel mind-boggling, but even at a low rate, a thirty-year loan ends up costing an awful lot in interest charges. This figure simply shows the total interest you'll pay as a percentage of the loan amount: If you borrow $100,000, and the total interest over thirty years amounts to $71,000, your TIP is 71 percent. The lower the number, the less you'll pay in overall interest should you keep the same loan for the entire term.

The loan estimate is an invaluable tool to help you understand and compare mortgages, which are pretty complicated financial instruments, in simplified, straightforward terms.

You can make the best apples-to-apples comparisons, however, when you're applying for the same type of loan from different lenders. So experts suggest figuring out what type of mortgage you want *first*. That means deciding whether you want a conventional mortgage or an FHA loan, for example, and determining the size of your down payment or whether you want to buy points.

If you can supply lenders with the same set of variables across the board, then their competing estimates will be even easier to compare.

WHY AND WHEN TO LOCK IN YOUR INTEREST RATE

Don't Let a Good One Get Away

At some point in your home search, even if you've never visited *Bloomberg*, *Kiplinger*, or *Bankrate*, and even if you've never read the business section of a newspaper in your entire life, you're likely to find yourself poring over interest rate data and pondering economist predictions in *The Wall Street Journal*.

Why? Once you've found the home you love, and a mortgage whose math you can live with, it's time to lock in your interest rate so that math doesn't suddenly change on you, leaving you high and dry.

Mortgage rates fluctuate constantly, and they could move significantly between the time you apply for a mortgage and the time you actually close on your home. While a drop in rates would make your mortgage more affordable, an increase could spell disaster if you're borrowing near the top of your price range—abruptly making the home you love too expensive to afford and derailing your entire home purchase (unless you can come up with the difference in cash). In short, once you locate a home you want to buy and a mortgage you can afford to buy it with, interest rate changes start to present a lot more risk than reward to a borrower.

That's why most lenders offer the opportunity to lock in an interest rate once you're approved for a mortgage—meaning they'll agree to honor that rate for a certain period, no matter what happens in the mortgage market. So if you qualify for a thirty-year mortgage at 3.75 percent, for example, you can choose to freeze that rate for forty-five days; then, even if rates rise to 4.25 percent or even 5.25 percent over the following few weeks, you'll still be able to get your 3.75 percent mortgage. But if rates fall—say, to 3.25 percent—you're still stuck at 3.75 percent.

As tempting as it may be to wait and watch in hopes that rates start to fall, which could save you a bit or even a bunch of money on your monthly payment, mortgage experts recommend locking in your interest rate as soon as the numbers work for your budget and you have a set closing date for the home purchase.

Once you're approved for a loan on a specific property, most lenders allow you to lock in a guaranteed rate for thirty, forty-five, or sixty days—long enough to get you to closing, and maybe a few days beyond, just in case. There can be a fee for this benefit, though it's often baked into your rate or other lender fees; a longer than normal rate-lock period will cost you more, however, as will an extension of your rate lock should your closing get delayed.

Buy Yourself Time

Once you have a closing date, count backward to determine how long a rate-lock period you need. Be sure to leave yourself a cushion of at least a few extra days in the event that something unexpectedly postpones the closing at the last minute.

Ask your lender what kind of fees, if any, are involved in a thirty-, forty-five-, and sixty-day rate lock, and what kind of fees they charge for an extension if your closing gets pushed back. Also make sure to ask if there are any situations where a rate lock agreement could be voided—for example, if your credit or income changes before closing.

While a lock-in prevents your rate from going up *or* down, some lenders might also allow you to take advantage of a one-time "float down." This perk offers you the best of both worlds: Your quoted rate won't go up, but if rates drop before your closing date, you get one chance to snag a lower interest rate. A float down may cost extra, so make sure you think it's worth the fee.

Either way, if you've successfully signed a contract to buy a home, and your ability to afford that home hinges on getting a particular mortgage rate, it's a very good idea to lock in that rate when you have the chance. It's a good idea to keep an eye on rate fluctuations, so you feel like you're making a sound decision—but remember that not even the world's top economists can predict interest rate movements with any great certainty. You don't want to lose out on your dream home because you held out for an extra eighth of a percentage point.

Chapter 5

Assembling Your Team

Between the intimidating cost, complicated contracts, financial fine print, and high stakes involved, buying a home can be a real challenge. Fortunately, it's not one you have to face alone. Once you've got your finances squared away, it's time to assemble your home buying team.

In this chapter, you'll meet the real estate and financial professionals who will help guide you through this complex process. You'll learn which pros are fully dedicated to your best interests, which ones may have shared loyalty, and the important role each plays in getting you through the door of your new home.

WHO'S ON YOUR SIDE?

Meet Your Home Buying Allies

There's nothing that says you *can't* buy a home all by yourself, with just your own wits and cash to support you. Some experienced real estate investors have both the financial means and the real estate training or legal expertise they need to buy and sell their own properties without hiring outside help. But for the rest of us? Help is greatly appreciated, and largely necessary.

Assembling and working with a core team of professionals can help ensure your home buying experience is a successful one. Here's a brief overview of the key players who will help you find, tour, evaluate, negotiate, finance, and purchase your home. We'll explain more about each service provider's specific role, and how to find a good one, throughout this chapter.

When to Go It Alone

Unless you're an experienced house flipper, a licensed Realtor, or a real estate attorney, you generally ought to employ the services of a buyer's agent. However, some buyers may not need one—for example, if you're purchasing a home from a family member, or buying a new home directly from the builder. Even in these instances, though, it's a good idea to have a real estate attorney or other professional review the contracts you're signing.

- **Real estate agent:** From arranging showings to writing and negotiating offers and contracts on your behalf, your real estate agent is the captain of your home buying team. An experienced buyer's agent will look out for you and you alone, representing your best interests through the entire process, from open house to closing—and generally at no cost to you, which we'll explain in the next section. Realtors are connected to other local real estate professionals, too, so they can also help you find other members of your team. Unless you're a licensed real estate agent yourself, there's almost no reason to forego using a buyer's agent.

- **Loan officer or mortgage broker:** You'll probably never meet the mortgage mathematician who will underwrite your loan, but you'll have plenty of contact with your loan officer. This will be your main point person at whatever bank or lender you choose to work with. You'll be sharing sensitive financial information with this person, and they'll be responsible for getting your loan application in the best shape possible before it goes to underwriting—so you want someone both trustworthy and competent.

- **Home inspector:** You would try on a new jacket before buying it, right? Well, a home costs about two thousand times more, and you can't really return it to the store once you buy it. So once you've had an offer accepted on a home, you'll want to have this major purchase of yours evaluated inside and out before signing away hundreds of thousands of dollars. Your home inspector will take a critical eye to the property, looking for any signs of rot, leaks, faulty wiring, or other issues that could potentially cause costly safety or structural problems.

- **Insurance agent:** An independent insurance agent can help you shop around for the best and most economical homeowner's insurance policy, and recommend any additional coverage you may need based on the home's location or condition.

- **Real estate attorney:** Many states require a real estate attorney to review and handle all closing paperwork to make sure the transaction goes smoothly. If your home purchase has any unusual clauses or financial mechanics—for example, if you offer to let the seller lease the home back from you for two weeks after closing, while they wait for their next home to be ready—you may want to hire an attorney to review your paperwork.

- **Housing counselor:** First-time buyers who feel especially unprepared or intimidated may want to seek the assistance of a housing counselor from a local nonprofit. A Housing and Urban Development–approved housing counselor can help you review and prepare your financial documents, explain different mortgage options and down payment assistance programs, and answer any questions you have about the home buying process at no charge to you. You can find a counselor in your area by entering your zip code online at www.consumerfinance.gov/find-a-housing-counselor/.

- **Family and friends:** Finally, don't forget your fan club—friends and family can be a big help. If any of your friends or family members purchased a home in the past few years, ask them for recommendations and advice. They may have a trusted Realtor or a home inspector they swear by, or some hindsight you could learn from. Even if they purchased a few towns away, their real estate agent may have a recommendation for an agent in your area. Family members who work in construction can offer realistic advice about what it will cost to rehab a fixer-upper or whether a structural issue should be a deal breaker. And those who have owned their homes for a while will no doubt have a helpful roster of recommended tradespeople, from plumbers to painters, which will come in handy as you settle into your new home.

WORKING WITH A BUYER'S AGENT

The Captain of Your Team

About nine out of ten home buyers used a real estate agent in 2020, according to the National Association of Realtors' Profile of Home Buyers and Sellers, and it's no wonder: As a buyer, there's almost no reason not to.

In most cases, the seller pays all real estate sales commissions, which are then split between the seller's agent and the buyer's agent. So working with a buyer's agent—who is legally, ethically committed to serving your best interests—is essentially free.

Perhaps because buyers aren't paying for the service (at least not directly), they don't tend to expend much time or effort choosing a real estate agent. According to that same report, 73 percent of buyers work with the first agent they talk to. Some people may feel a social obligation to work with a friend or a cousin who just got their real estate license.

But your agent is perhaps the single most important person to have in your corner as you make what is likely the biggest purchase of your life. This isn't a job for just anyone. Think about it this way: If you were playing in the World Series or the Super Bowl, would you want the first person who shows up with a clipboard to coach your team?

There's no substitute for a good buyer's agent, whose primary role is that of a trusted advisor. An experienced buyer's agent can help you make sense of the local housing market, put prices into context, avoid costly missteps, and navigate the contractual jargon and complexities inherent in buying a home. When the time comes, they'll guide you through the confusing paperwork, negotiate on your behalf, and write sales contracts that protect your interests.

But you also want someone you click with on a personal level, because house hunting can be an emotional and all-consuming endeavor. You'll be in regular contact with this person pretty much daily for the next few weeks or months, and you may share some difficult setbacks, like getting outbid on your dream home.

In short, you're going to be spending a lot of time with this person, and potentially leaning on them for more than just real estate advice. It's important that you like and trust your agent, and that they make themselves available to you when you need them.

HOW TO FIND A GOOD REAL ESTATE AGENT

So how do you find this all-important member of your team? Here are some ways to begin your search. Once you've found a few potential candidates, experts recommend meeting with at least three real estate agents before committing to work with one of them.

- **Word of mouth:** If you have friends, family members, or neighbors who recently bought a home, ask whether they would recommend their real estate agent. If your peers had a good experience with someone, and your situations are fairly similar—for example, if your friends bought a condo, and you're also looking for a condo in the same price range or area—that's a promising starting point.

- **Online reviews:** It's wise to approach online ratings with a bit of skepticism, since friends, employees, or rivals can post misleading fake reviews. But when someone has dozens of testimonials and loads of positive feedback on *Zillow, Yelp, Angi,* or another review site, that's a pretty good sign.
- **The capital *R*:** While the terms are often used interchangeably, not all real estate agents are Realtors. The capital *R* refers to a member of the National Association of Realtors, which means the agent has sworn to uphold the organization's ethical principles and has met continuing education standards and other requirements.
- **Community expertise:** Look for an agent who's active in the community you want to purchase in. Agents with deep local roots have street-level neighborhood knowledge, are well connected to local lenders and other real estate professionals, and may learn about new listings long before they turn up online.
- **Responsiveness:** When you reach out to a real estate agent, do it in the medium you're most comfortable communicating in—whether that's text, phone, or email. Some agents are quick to return a text but rarely respond to emails; others prefer to call on the phone, regardless of how you contacted them. You want to know that, as the pace of your home search intensifies—when you're waiting to hear back on an offer, or you have an urgent question—you'll have an open line of quick, convenient communication with your Realtor.
- **Beware of dual agency and transaction brokers:** Most real estate agents work with a range of different clients, including both home buyers and sellers. Ordinarily, that's fine, but it can become an issue if your buyer's agent (or their brokerage) is also representing the seller of the home you want to purchase. This

is known as dual agency, and while it's legal in most states, it could potentially cloud the loyalty of your agent, since they're representing two sides of the same transaction. You can avoid this by working with a "buyers only" agent—someone who exclusively represents home buyers—or simply choosing someone who mostly represents buyers, or specializes in assisting first-time home buyers. Some agents, meanwhile, work as "transaction brokers," meaning their only loyalty is to a smooth sale, not necessarily to you. (This is common in Florida, where agents are presumed to be transaction brokers unless a single-agent relationship is established in writing.)

What Is a Buyer's Agent Agreement?

When you settle on a buyer's broker that you'd like to work with, you'll typically sign a buyer's agent agreement. This document details the terms of your working relationship—that, in exchange for representing you, the agent will receive the buyer's agent commission for any home you purchase with his or her help over a set period of time, typically three to six months.

It's fairly straightforward, but still worth reading the fine print. In an *exclusive* buyer's agent agreement, for example, the agent could be owed a commission even if you end up buying a home through a different broker, if the sale takes place within the determined time frame.

FINDING A GOOD LENDER

What to Look For in a Loan Officer

Now that you've found your real estate agent—your star player, so to speak—it's time to fill out the rest of your roster, starting with your lender. After all, someone has to bankroll this team!

If you're not already working with a lender, ask your Realtor to recommend a loan officer who's experienced with first-time home buyer loans. Your agent wants you to succeed—that's the only way they'll get paid, after all. So if they're able to set you up with a lender they know and trust, who has a proven track record of getting first-time buyers across the financial finish line, they'll be more than happy to do so.

This doesn't mean you're obligated to work with that lender, however. With so much money at stake, it's worth shopping around for a mortgage that best meets your specific needs—whether you want the lowest possible interest rate, the smallest possible down payment, or the highest borrowing limit you can find. Here are some things to consider when choosing a lender.

- **Check your state's housing finance agency:** First-time home buyer programs can differ from ordinary mortgages, and some lenders are more familiar with these loans than others. If you're interested in a first-time home buyer loan offered through your state's housing finance agency—and these are well worth investigating—check their website for a list of approved lenders. These financial institutions know the drill: They won't be put off by a small down payment, and they'll be better equipped to find a mortgage that fits your needs as a first-time buyer.

- **Start (but don't end) with your bank:** If you like your bank or credit union, there's no reason not to inquire about their loan rates. However, make sure you compare rates and fees with at least two other lenders. Just because you're happy with your checking account and the online banking features they offer doesn't mean they're a low-priced or responsive mortgage lender.
- **Or start with a loan officer:** If your Realtor, friends, or family members recommend a specific loan officer, that's a great place to start. No matter which lender you choose, you'll ultimately be working with a loan officer to apply for your mortgage. This person—formally called a mortgage loan originator—will be your primary point of contact at the financial institution, so make sure you feel confident in their ability to manage the many moving parts of your application. You'll want someone organized enough to meet all the required deadlines and experienced enough to suggest various ways to structure the loan to your advantage—all while patiently explaining the process to you in clear terms and directly answering any questions you may have.
- **Understand how mortgage brokers work:** While a loan officer works for a specific bank or lending institution, a mortgage broker is an independent (and often licensed) professional who can shop your application around to various lenders on your behalf. They can walk you through your options and help you compare different loan products from different banks. Mortgage brokers receive a fee for this service, however, amounting to 1 percent to 2 percent of the loan, paid by either you or the lender. And because you're putting one person in control of all your lending options, you'll want to research online reviews, check whether they meet state licensing requirements, and interview potential mortgage brokers before choosing to work with one.

- **Gauge responsiveness:** While you won't be in constant contact with your lender, things move fast once you have a home under contract, and not always during business hours. So it's important that your lender responds quickly when you need them to. If you send them an email at 8 p.m., do they get back to you right away as a matter of habit? Or at least first thing in the morning?
- **Compare loan estimates:** As mentioned in Chapter 4, lenders must provide you with a simple, three-page loan estimate once you apply for a mortgage on a specific property. This is your best and final opportunity to evaluate what each lender is offering and which one you want to work with. By this time, you should be able to compare not just the interest rates and fees on the loan estimate but also your experiences with each lender thus far. Was the application process simple and efficient? Did you have to hound the loan officer for responses to your questions? Did they make any careless errors, like putting a typo in your name? Make sure you feel confident in your lender's ability to get you across the goal line.

A Lender's Loyalty

One last thing to note: While a good loan officer acts as your advocate within the financial institution, and can and should be a huge help to you, lenders are ultimately most concerned with protecting themselves from risk. So aside from the customer service it takes to win your business, you shouldn't expect your lender to have your back in quite the same way that you can expect your buyer's agent to look out for you.

HIRING A HOME INSPECTOR, INSURANCE AGENT, AND ATTORNEY

Rounding Out Your Roster

The rest of your home buying team enters the picture a bit later—generally after you've had an offer accepted on a home. However, it's not a bad idea to research and reach out to these folks well before you need them, since things start to move pretty quickly once a home goes under contract.

THE HOME INSPECTOR

Once a seller accepts your offer, you'll generally have a set period of time—typically a week to ten days—to perform a home inspection. We'll cover the home inspection process in detail in Chapter 9, but essentially, this is your one chance to get an objective assessment of a home before you pour your life savings into it. It's important to make the most of this opportunity.

Like a buyer's agent, your home inspector is 100 percent on your side, though you pay for the service directly and upfront. Your inspector will tour the property inside and out, casting a critical eye on everything from the site grade and foundation to the roof and plumbing fixtures. The inspector's report will note any safety, structural, or cosmetic concerns—and potentially save you from dumping hundreds of thousands of dollars into a money pit.

Here are some things to look for in a home inspector:

- **Referrals:** Once again, a referral from friends, family, or a real estate agent is perhaps the best way to find a good home inspector. (Though keep in mind, your agent has a vested interest in getting the sale to close; given that a home inspector is looking for reasons *not* to buy the home, that could create a minor conflict of interest.)
- **Experience:** The longer a home inspector has been in business, the better. You also want someone who's familiar with the common types of construction found in your area, and well versed in the style and period of home you're buying. You probably wouldn't take a Subaru to a BMW mechanic, for example—so if you're buying a 150-year-old farmhouse, make sure your home inspector has plenty of experience with old single-family homes, not just condos or twenty-first-century construction.
- **Sample reports:** Ask a home inspector for a sample of a recent inspection report, and see how much detail is provided. Do the comments read like generic-sounding checklist items, or do they get into nitty-gritty, useful detail? Are there photos included, with explanatory captions? Does the report provide maintenance suggestions or a punch list of repairs? The more granular the detail, the better.
- **Licenses and accreditations:** Most, but not all, states require home inspectors to be licensed. There are also professional accrediting organizations that a home inspector may belong to, such as the American Society of Home Inspectors (ASHI). Such accreditations don't guarantee an attentive inspection, but they're worth checking up on. Meanwhile, some inspectors are also licensed architects, retired engineers, or former contractors who can bring even more valuable insights to your inspection.

Even New Construction Warrants an Inspection

You might assume that only older properties and fixer-uppers need a thorough home inspection, but inspectors find issues in brand-new homes all the time. Clearly the roof is new, but what if it wasn't installed correctly or up to code? Some inspectors report finding plumbing fixtures in newly built homes that weren't hooked up to drains, allowing water to flood the kitchen. You may offer to buy a house before final touches are installed, like switch plates for the lights—and in that case, your inspector can create a comprehensive punch list of outstanding issues the seller or builder needs to remedy before closing.

THE INSURANCE AGENT

We'll also take a more thorough look at homeowner's insurance in Chapter 9, but this is another service you'll need to shop for before closing. In fact, your lender won't finalize your home loan until they see proof of insurance coverage (called the binder).

If this is your first home, you're probably going to want to work with an insurance agent, who can walk you through what's required and explain where you might want more or less coverage. An agent can also help you secure flood insurance if it's required or coverage for earthquakes and other types of hazards not normally included in a standard homeowner's policy. Here are some tips for finding an insurance agent:

- **Start with your car insurer:** Insurance companies offer big discounts to customers who bundle their policies. If you're pleased with your car insurance company, it's worth asking them for a home insurance quote. While it's possible to apply directly online, it's often worth speaking to an agent who can assess your insurance needs and customize a policy for you.

- **Consider going independent:** Unlike a "captive agent" who works at an insurance company, an independent agent isn't affiliated with any one insurer. They can shop around for you, looking for the best combination of coverage and low premiums from a range of insurers. A local agent may also have a good feel for what type of coverage you need and which companies offer the most competitive rates in your area.

- **Compare quotes and check reviews:** Experts suggest getting at least three insurance quotes. But it's also important to check an insurer's customer satisfaction rating from an outfit like J.D. Power or Consumer Reports. Insurance isn't just about the lowest price—it's about feeling protected when you need it most. You don't want to be fighting over an insurance claim after you've just experienced the trauma of a house fire.

- **Ask your lender:** Your lender is likely to have opinions on insurance providers as well and may be able to recommend a local agent.

THE ATTORNEY

There's one more person you may need or want to hire before closing, and that's a real estate attorney. Some states require an attorney to oversee closing transactions, in which case you'll need to pay for a real estate lawyer to handle the process. The closing attorney coordinates the title insurance process, reviews and prepares documents such as the deed, and executes the final transaction by disbursing funds, among other things.

All of these services—which you're paying for in your closing costs—are a help to you, but the closing attorney is ultimately a neutral party who's representing the lender. So you may wish to hire that attorney (or a separate one) to do some work solely for you—especially if your real estate purchase is a very complicated or expensive one.

Some Realtors are better than others at customizing contracts and writing purchase agreements—some are former lawyers, in fact. But it doesn't hurt to have an attorney look over your purchase and sale agreement and other binding contracts with your interests in mind.

MEET THE OTHER TEAM

They're Not Your Opponents, Exactly—but They're Not Your Friends, Either

Before we move on, there are just a few more characters to introduce: those on the other side of the negotiating table.

These folks aren't necessarily your adversaries, though emotions and tempers can run high as closing day approaches. And in fact, a respectful working relationship can go a long way to making a home sale go more smoothly for everyone. But at the very least, the people below are likely to approach the sale with very different motives from yours.

The Seller

You may not meet the owner of the home you want to buy until closing, if at all; most of the back-and-forth will be handled by your respective real estate agents. That lack of visibility can allow some low-key animosity to brew, but remember that, in all likelihood, this person is just trying to get the best price for what is probably their biggest asset, with as few headaches or uncertainties as possible.

As stressful as this process is for you, it may be even more acutely emotional for the seller. Where you see the foundation of your future, they're grappling with letting go of their past—perhaps the place where they first fell in love with their spouse, lost a loved one, or raised their children (or even where they grew up themselves).

Sellers may also have secondary priorities beyond getting the highest sale price—like a desire to close quickly or to wait until they have a new home to move into before finalizing the sale. Your buyer's agent should try to find out what's important to the seller, because anything you or your agent can do to allay those concerns will ultimately make your offer more appealing and your transaction more successful. For example, if the seller needs to close before or after a specific date in order to finalize the purchase of their next home, you may have an advantage over other buyers if you can be flexible with your timing. Make sure your agent communicates that flexibility in your offer.

The Seller's Agent

Just as your real estate agent is required to act in your best interest, the listing agent has an obligation to serve his or her client: the seller. Listing agents still need to follow all fair housing laws and other ethics rules, such as disclosing known problems when asked about them. A listing agent can help your agent make a stronger offer if they're forthcoming about their seller's motives—for example, if they share that the seller wants a quick closing. But at the end of the day, the seller's agent is trying to get the best deal for his or her client.

Ask Pointed Questions

In most states, even if a listing agent doesn't have to volunteer negative information about a home—like any good salesperson, they're not going to lead their sales pitch with the thirty-year-old roof—they generally must answer questions about the home's condition truthfully, to the best of their knowledge. So when you're touring the home, ask direct questions about any concerns. They may not be able to answer every inquiry—"I don't know" may be a truthful response—but it doesn't hurt to ask.

The Home Appraiser

The home appraiser isn't exactly working *against* you—in fact, you're the one who has to pay for their services, and you generally won't meet this person, and ideally won't devote a whole lot of attention to their role in the home sale. However, the appraisal can sometimes throw a late-stage monkey wrench into your home purchase.

As you learned in Chapter 4, lenders require a third-party appraisal of a property's fair market value before they will fork over hundreds of thousands of dollars. They are, in a sense, business partners with you until you pay off the mortgage, so they want to be sure they're not overpaying for the property. If they're lending you $300,000 to buy a $330,000 home, they want to ensure the place is really worth $330,000, and that they're not taking on more risk than they expected.

The potential problem is this: When you're purchasing the home with a low down payment, there's not a lot of wiggle room if the official appraisal comes in lower than the sale price.

In our earlier example, say the appraiser—who by law isn't made aware of the agreed-upon price—files an appraisal report estimating the home's value at $310,000, or $20,000 below the sale price. That throws the lender's delicate calculations all out of whack: Suddenly, they're financing almost the entire appraised value of the home, not the 90 percent that they signed up for.

What that means to you as a buyer is that you'll either need to come up with another $20,000 in cash before closing, reconfigure the mortgage (perhaps at a worse rate), or renegotiate a lower price with the seller. We'll explain more about the appraisal process, and how to handle a low appraisal, in Chapter 9.

Chapter 6

Location, Location, Location

No doubt you've heard the saying, *The three most important things in real estate are location, location, location.* There's a lot of truth to that old adage. With enough time and money, you can change virtually anything and everything about your home—except where it is.

In this chapter, we'll look at why location is such an important factor in any real estate purchase, how the neighborhood you live in can impact your quality of life, how to gauge a community's personality if you don't already live there, and what to look for in an individual home site.

WHY LOCATION IS THE GOLDEN RULE OF REAL ESTATE

You Can't Buy It at the Hardware Store

Why might a Craftsman bungalow in California sell for five times the price of a similar home in Kansas or South Dakota? Why may a tiny Manhattan condo fetch a higher sales price than a five-bedroom Victorian in upstate New York? Because when it comes to purchasing property, you're not just buying a building—you're buying the land beneath it too.

Even when purchasing a condominium—where your direct ownership interest is confined to the interior of your unit—you're still purchasing shared rights to a parcel of land. Where that land is located has everything to do with home prices. In some high-cost housing markets, more than half of a home's price can be attributed to the value of the land beneath it, according to a 2019 Redfin study of assessed property values.

Consider a single-family house, maybe a three-bedroom colonial, in the Cleveland metro area. The price of a typical house in Cleveland has risen about 45 percent since 2000, according to the Case-Shiller US National Home Price Index, which tracks repeat home sales in twenty different markets across the country. Now consider a similar three-bedroom colonial in Boston, a metro area that has benefitted from a twenty-first-century boom in the biotech, healthcare, and higher education industries. The price of that typical Boston-area single-family home has leaped by about 158 percent in that same period—more than three times as much.

A lot of factors influence housing prices, and almost all of them are local or regional in nature:

- **Job market:** Historically, the availability of jobs (and how well they pay) has been the leading determinant in a region's home prices. People migrate to economically dynamic areas in search of opportunity. Once there, higher wages support higher home prices. Booming job markets have helped home prices skyrocket in areas like San Francisco; Seattle; Boston; New York; Washington, DC; and Austin, Texas; over the past decade. Some experts expect this effect to lessen as more people work remotely in a post-pandemic economy—but not disappear entirely. Pay attention to where the job growth is if you want to find the next housing boom.
- **Home inventory:** You're probably aware of the law of supply and demand: When there's more supply of a good than buyer demand for it, prices will go down, and when demand outstrips supply, prices go up. This fundamental economic principle applies to homes as well. Areas that restrict new construction or face geographic limits to expansion are often unable to build enough housing to keep up with demand—and demand increases when there are lots of good jobs to be had or lots of desirable amenities. If a hundred buyers are vying for fifty available homes, that competition will naturally push up prices.
- **Transit and infrastructure:** Regional investments in public transit, roads, sidewalks, and utilities influence home buyer decisions and real estate values as well. For example, buyers and renters alike place a premium on public transit. A 2019 study by the National Association of Realtors found that homes near transit stations sold at a 4 percent to 24 percent premium over similar homes, and commanded higher rents too.
- **Natural environment:** It's no secret that Americans, especially retirees, have been shifting southward to the Sun Belt in recent

years. Some of that migration is the result of thriving job markets in more affordable cities such as Austin and Atlanta, but many northern emigrants are also tempted by snow-free winters. Meanwhile, properties on or near a body of water generally sell for a premium, as do urban homes that are closer to parks and green space.

- **School districts:** Not all home buyers have or want to have kids. But those who do want to know that their children will get a quality education in a safe, nurturing environment. Anecdotally, real estate agents will tell you that homes in well-regarded school districts hold their values better during good times and bad. Data seem to bear this out, too: One study, updated in 2021, found that for every per-pupil dollar invested in local schools, home values increased by $20. Another study found that after the state of Florida began grading its public schools in 1999, Gainesville homes near an A-rated school received a nearly $10,000 bump in value over similar homes near a B-rated school.

- **Rental demand:** Neighborhoods near universities, big hospitals, or other economic engines that draw in a steady influx of new residents typically experience consistent rental demand. That in turn can help support nearby home prices, since homeowners and investors alike know they can rent out a property for as much or more than they're paying on it.

The Proximity Premium

A 2017 study by the real estate brokerage Redfin found that for every one point increase in a home's Transit Score—a rating system that measures proximity to public transit options—its sales price increased an average of more than $2,000.

A Good Location Is Subjective Too

It's important to remember that, first and foremost, you're buying a home for you. If you don't have or expect to have kids, it probably doesn't make sense for you to pay more money just to be near a top-rated elementary school. If you no longer need to commute to an office, then perhaps there's no sense in paying a premium to be near the subway.

Yet if you're approaching your home purchase as an investment, then on some level, you're also buying with someone else in mind—the person you might sell this home to in five or fifteen years. In that sense, choosing a location that other buyers will likely value can help ensure your home holds or increases its value.

TAKE A COMMUNITY-FIRST APPROACH IN YOUR HOME SEARCH

Prioritize Place over Property

Relocation experts recommend shopping for a community before searching for specific homes, and the reason is simple: inertia. As Newton's First Law of Motion states, an object at rest tends to stay at rest unless acted upon by an outside force. Once you settle into a place and plant some roots, it can feel increasingly difficult to pick up and move, absent a massive life change.

For one thing, moving is almost always a stressful experience. In a recent North American Van Lines survey of Americans who had moved in the past three years, 64 percent said their recent move was *one of the most stressful experiences in their entire lives*. Most people need a pretty compelling motivation to bother moving and otherwise will tend to stay put. The longer they do so, the more "stuff" they tend to accumulate, making it that much more daunting to pack it all up.

Even if you do summon the will to change homes, escaping the gravitational field of your chosen community can be even trickier as time goes on.

The longer you live somewhere, the more relationships you start to develop in the community. Maybe you join a volunteer group or get involved in a local church or fitness club. Before you know it, you may have kids in the school system or involved in youth sports. That's when you realize that while moving just one town away wouldn't really change your commute or climate, it could strain or sever some of your friendships or those of your children. As one relocation expert put it, "It's easier to update your kitchen than to change your school district."

Of course, you can always change your mind later and move to a new community—people do it all the time. It just gets harder to do as time goes on. So "Where" is the type of decision you want to get right the first time, if at all possible.

THE IMPORTANCE OF PLACE

The states and communities we live in—and even the neighborhoods we occupy within those towns and cities—have an outsized influence over our daily lives and those of our children.

Your choice of state, for example, could determine whether you have to pay sales or income taxes or how robust your healthcare options are, among other things. It could also influence how long you live: Average life expectancy can differ by a matter of years, even between nearby states. Residents of New York can expect to live 2.4 years longer than their neighbors in Pennsylvania, for example, according to data from the Centers for Disease Control and Prevention (CDC).

Live Long and Prosper

According to CDC data, the states with the highest average life expectancy at birth as of 2018 were Hawaii (age 81), California (80.8), New York (80.5), Minnesota (80.5), Connecticut (80.4), Massachusetts (80.1), Washington (80), and Colorado (80). The states with the lowest life expectancy were Arkansas (75.6), Oklahoma (75.6), Louisiana (75.6), Tennessee (75.5), Kentucky (75.3), Alabama (75.1), Mississippi (74.6), and West Virginia (74.4).

The community you choose within that state, meanwhile, could determine how much of your life you spend commuting to work, the types of restaurants and entertainment available to you, or whether your kids will have access to free preschool or other enrichment programs.

It's not just big-picture stuff, either. Your location can affect your day-to-day existence for years to come. In some communities, curbside trash pickup and recycling are included in your property taxes; in others, you'll have to pay extra for that service, or potentially even spend your Saturdays hauling your own refuse to the dump. Some towns benefit from a strong commercial tax base of office and retail centers that pump money into community coffers and help to fund schools, parks, libraries, and other municipal services; others rely almost exclusively on homeowners to pay the bills.

Finally, even which neighborhood you choose within a given community can play an important role in shaping your life. Your neighborhood and how close it is to a highway, industrial zone, or power plant can determine the quality of the air you breathe and thus whether you or your kids face a greater likelihood of developing asthma or other respiratory issues. Crime rates and safety can vary dramatically by just a few city blocks. Your home address can determine whether you'll be able to walk to places like shops, restaurants, parks, and friends' homes—as well as which schools your children (or future children) have access to.

Harvard University economist Raj Chetty, director of the nonprofit Opportunity Insights, has spent years studying the role neighborhoods play in children's lives. That research has helped create the Opportunity Atlas, which maps census tracts with the greatest social and economic mobility—places where children from low-income households have a greater chance of rising out of poverty in adulthood.

Neighborhoods are so important that, according to Opportunity Insights, every extra year of childhood spent living in a high-mobility neighborhood directly results in better outcomes in adulthood—from higher incomes and college graduation rates to lower incarceration rates.

Right now, you probably have at least some idea of where you'd like to buy—whether it's near your job, family members, or your current home. But even within a metro area or a single community, it's worth taking a deep look at which neighborhoods—and even which particular streets—feel most like home to you. In the next two sections, we'll look at some ways to research potential neighborhoods and get to know a place before you decide to move there.

HOW TO SCOUT AND RESEARCH NEIGHBORHOODS

Getting the Feel for a Place When You Don't Already Live There

The best way to get a sense of a neighborhood's livability is, well, living there. So your location search ought to start with the places you know best: where you live now and any places you've lived in the past. Also think about how you've felt when visiting friends and family members—and ask them whether your impressions of their neighborhoods align with their own experience.

BROADEN YOUR HORIZONS, THEN SLOWLY NARROW THEM

But that's just a starting point. You want to cast a wide net at first—don't yet rule out places you're unfamiliar with—and slowly refine your search.

Consider what matters most to you in terms of proximity. Do you want to be within a certain commuting radius of your job or near certain family members? Or is it more important that you live in a woodsy or rural area, with access to nature, or in a bustling urban village, with plenty of shops and restaurants you can walk to? You want to feel safe at home, so you may cross off areas with high violent crime rates. Then, of course, there's the matter of price: Where are the communities that you can actually afford to buy into?

For most people, the ideal community would serve many of these wishes at once. You may want a place that combines abundant green space with a thriving shopping and dining district; where you can get a house with a yard, while still being within walking distance of a subway line—all for a price you can afford.

Unless your budget is beyond limit, though, there are bound to be trade-offs. Think hard about what is most important to you (your locational needs), and what would be nice to have but not completely necessary (your wants). Then start researching and touring communities that meet your most crucial requirements.

If commute time is a major concern, look at the obvious candidates: communities located along major highways, subway lines, and bus routes that can get you door to door without much trouble. But also open up your mind (and *Google Maps*) to consider towns in your metro area that you've never devoted much thought to before. Even towns that appear drab as you drive through them can hide enchanting enclaves you may not be able to see from the highway.

Follow the spidery spokes of major roads and railroad lines on the map, and ponder places you've seen on subway signs but never in person. You can use an app such as TravelTime (app.traveltime .com) to create a custom commuting radius by mode of transport. For example, you can enter the address of your workplace, and see what areas fall within a thirty-minute drive—or bike ride, train trip, or walk—of that location.

Then start narrowing down the options. Price is an obvious winnowing strategy. Some desirable towns can be off-the-charts expensive. Read community profiles online and check school district ratings (along with other online resources, which we discuss in the next section). Ask friends or colleagues about towns they're familiar with, whether they grew up there or live there now.

Consider geographical features. Have you always dreamed of living near the water or a state park with hiking trails? Would you thrill to the idea of living along a bike path or down the street from a skating pond or swimming hole? Some communities offer these features, and some don't.

Also think about cultural assets. Do you want to live somewhere with a thriving art, music, or restaurant scene? Is there a vibrant immigrant population that would make you feel welcome and supported? Is there a college in town, and if so, would that make an area feel young and vibrant to you or a little too much like a frat party? Every community has something to offer, with its own pros and cons—it's a matter of finding one that fits your idea of home.

Life on the Edge

Something to keep in the back of your mind: Properties on the outskirts of town, particularly where one community or county borders another, can be more susceptible to new development. When officials or developers are looking for a spot to put, say, a proposed gas pipeline or trash incinerator, they often look first to the very edge of town.

POUND THE PAVEMENT

Once you've narrowed things down to a handful of communities, start visiting them in person. Drive or walk around the streets, looking for tranquil and charming neighborhoods. Spend an afternoon in a park, pop into a local coffee shop—even try doing some day-to-day errands, like grocery shopping—and take mental notes to get a feel for each place.

Ask people you meet what it's like to live there and what they love about the community. Candid conversations with locals can provide some of the best intel you'll get; you may learn about beloved block party traditions or even get tips on homes about to come on the market.

But even if you're bashful, a simple look around can tell you plenty. If it's an election year, the presence or lack of yard signs can tell you how politically engaged a community is. The contents of those signs, meanwhile, may tell you the political leanings of your potential neighbors and thus how likely they might be to, say, support a tax increase to pay for a new school or library.

Are the streets full of potholes, or in pretty good condition? Are the playgrounds, basketball courts, and baseball fields well maintained?

Are the streets and yards bare and sun baked, or are there towering trees casting shade? Mature trees not only raise nearby property values; they also lower cooling costs, help prevent flooding and soil erosion, and purify the air—so they're nice to have around. If there aren't many mature street trees in a neighborhood, do you at least spot some new saplings being tended to—the mark of a city that's investing in its future?

Most important, as you walk around, ask yourself if you feel comfortable there. Because once the data-driven decisions have whittled down your list, you're really just looking to answer the most important question of all: Do you feel at home? Could you picture yourself living here?

The Fair Isaac Corporation (FICO) pioneered the concept of the credit score, which mortgage lenders use as a shorthand measure of a borrower's creditworthiness. Your credit score is a numerical snapshot of your credit history at a moment in time, and reflects information on file with the three credit bureaus—Experian, Equifax, and TransUnion—such as any late or missed payments. The higher your FICO score, the more (and better) mortgage options you'll have available.

Photo credit: © Coolcaesar
via Wikimedia Commons

THINGS THAT BOOST YOUR CREDIT SCORE

Have open, active accounts in good standing

Diversify your credit accounts

Pay all your bills on time

Reduce your debt balances

Get rid of negative information on your credit report

300

850

Building a good credit score (something in the 700s or 800s) takes time and consistency, but it can mean the difference between getting the best mortgage rate or a more expensive loan—or not qualifying for a mortgage at all. These steps can help prospective home buyers raise their credit score.

What Do You Need to
BUY A HOUSE?

1 **MORTGAGE PRE-APPROVAL**
If you're not purchasing a home with cash, you'll need a mortgage pre-approval.

2 **EARNEST MONEY**
This proves to the sellers that you "earnestly" want to buy their house.

3 **MONEY FOR DOWN PAYMENT**
Most down payments are 3%–10% of the sale price.

4 **MONEY FOR CLOSING COSTS**
Mortgage closing costs are typically 1%–4% of the loan amount.

5 **MONEY TO HIRE AN INSPECTOR**
An inspector will help determine if there are problems with the home before you buy.

As this chart shows, there are significant cash costs (earnest money, down payment, and so on) associated with purchasing a home. While some can be negotiated—for instance, the size of the down payment—the prospective buyer will need to have cash on hand to cover these expenses. For this reason, many home buyers spend a few years accumulating enough cash to ensure they can cover each cost associated with home buying.

In some cases, low- and moderate-income buyers purchasing a home in a rural area can obtain a no-down-payment housing loan from the Department of Agriculture. The home must be the borrower's primary residence, among other requirements. For more information on how to qualify for such a loan, go to www.usda.gov.

Homeowner's insurance is designed to offer the homeowner financial relief in the event of major damage, whether from flood, fire, or storm. In most purchases, it is mandatory; the lender will not authorize a home buying loan unless the prospective buyer can show proof of homeowner's insurance.

If a homeowner fails to make their mortgage payments, their lender can foreclose upon the property—repossessing the home and reselling it, often at a below-market price. However, first-time buyers should approach such properties with caution. Foreclosed homes may have significant damage or deferred maintenance that can be costly to address.

Photo credit: © Getty Images/fstop123

Most home buyers purchase an existing home, but some choose new construction—and others custom-build their own home on a lot of land. This can be expensive and time-consuming, but it ensures the buyer will get the home they want, adapted to their particular needs. Building from scratch typically requires securing a construction loan and surveying the land for suitability.

Photo credit: © Getty Images/sculpies

IS BUYING A FIXER-UPPER RIGHT FOR YOU?

A deal on a house that needs some TLC can be great. But here's what you should consider:

SET YOUR BUDGET

How much are you willing to spend?

CONSIDER YOUR LOCATION

How much the home's value will increase is limited by its neighborhood.

INSPECT THE PROPERTY

The cost of the home plus the cost of repairs shouldn't exceed the market value of other houses in the area.

INVESTIGATE LOAN OPTIONS

Conventional loans may not work for a fixer-upper. And a good credit score is essential when considering other possibilities.

A house that's in need of many repairs and renovations may be offered at a substantially lower price, but buyers should make sure they have the necessary cash and time to pay for the work to make the home livable—a process that may take many months, depending on the number and type of repairs needed.

They don't build 'em like they used to, and that's a good and bad thing. Historic or antique homes can offer unmatched character and timeless craftsmanship. However, many of these homes were built before the existence of modern building codes, so if an older home hasn't been thoroughly updated, it could contain outdated wiring, lead paint, asbestos, or other hazards. Local historic districts may also limit what changes can be made to an antique property.

Photo credit: © Getty Images/VickyRu

President Franklin D. Roosevelt signed the Servicemen's Readjustment Act of 1944, better known as the GI Bill. This legislation offered a variety of benefits to veterans of World War II, including low-cost housing mortgages. The bill has been updated a number of times to reflect changing history, and today such low-cost housing loans are available to veterans through the Department of Veterans Affairs.

Photo credit: © Public domain, via Wikimedia Commons

The Great Depression (1929–39) and subsequent economic downturns drove many Americans to hunger and homelessness. Many jobless workers gathered at soup kitchens and struggled to find housing. Home buying sank dramatically, and the housing crisis in the US was not fully resolved until the end of World War II, when the economy stabilized.

Photo credit: © National Archives at College Park, Public domain, via Wikimedia Commons

TOP 8 ISSUES FOUND IN HOME INSPECTIONS

1

ELECTRICAL

Look for visible signs of outdated wiring. Make sure outlets are properly grounded. Test light switches to ensure they work properly.

2

WATER & PLUMBING

Drippy faucets, leaking pipes, and signs of water damage can point to bigger problems such as mold or costly plumbing repairs.

3

HVAC

Replace filters as needed. An inspector will test the heating and cooling system, and the thermostat, to ensure all is in good working order.

4

SMOKE & CARBON MONOXIDE

Smoke and carbon monoxide detectors need to be in working condition.

5

WINDOWS

Windows should open and close freely and be free of cracks and fogging between panes.

6

PESTS

Visual signs of pests should be investigated for signs of infestation. Treatment and repair may be required.

7

FOUNDATION

Cracks in foundation walls, basement water intrusion, and uneven flooring can point to foundation issues.

8

DOORS

Doors should open, close, and lock properly. Garage doors must have working safety features.

A thorough home inspection should catch all of the possible issues shown here, as well as others that may be more hidden. For this reason, a good home inspector is a worthwhile investment. The home inspector will examine all of the home's systems (e.g., heat, roofing, electrical wiring) and determine if any of them are in immediate need of repair.

HOW LONG WILL IT LAST?

Average Life and Replacement Cost of Your Home's Major Systems and Appliances

7 DISHWASHER
5–10 Years
$400–$1,000

8 VENTING
20–30 Years
$500–$1,500

9 RANGE/STOVE
15–20 Years
$600–$2,000

10 WASHER/ DRYER
1–15 Years
$500–$1,500 *EACH*

11 FURNACE/ HEATER
15–20 Years
$2,500–$7,500

12 WATER HEATER
10–15 Years
$800–$1,600

13 CENTRAL AIR CONDITIONING
10–20 Years
$4,000–$8,000

1 ROOF
15–25 Years
$5,000–$20,000

2 EXTERIOR PAINT
4–10 Years
$2,000–$10,000

3 WINDOWS
10–40 Years
$500–$1,500 *EACH*

4 REFRIGERATOR
15–20 Years
$800–$2,000

5 GARBAGE DISPOSAL
8–12 Years
$150–$350

6 MICROWAVE
5–10 Years
$100–$500

Every home system or appliance has an expected lifespan, after which it will have to be repaired or replaced—though some features, such as wood floors or stone counters, can be expected to last a lifetime. Here are some of the more common home repairs and replacement purchases you may need to make over the course of your home's lifespan. Costs will vary dramatically by region.

SCOUTING FROM A DISTANCE

Using Census Data, Flood Maps, and Other Helpful Resources

Nothing can really replicate an in-person visit, but if you're relocating from another state or simply want to narrow down your options remotely before doing any on-the-ground research, there are plenty of methods to gain a feel for a community online. Here are some helpful tools to research a place from afar.

Google Street View

Take a virtual "drive" through different communities using the Street View feature on *Google Maps*. Cruise along various streets, including main commercial corridors and residential side streets, and you'll be treated to a virtual treasure trove of information.

Are there sidewalks and street trees? Are there kids playing in the streets, and swing sets in the yards? Do the homes, yards, and storefronts look well kept or neglected? Which streets appear to have lots of traffic? Do all the houses look the same, or is there an interesting mix of architecture?

Census Data

The US Census can provide you with incredibly granular data about a neighborhood, zip code, or community. You can find what percentage of residents have a college degree and how many speak a different language at home. You can compare age ranges and relationship data to see whether a neighborhood is full of middle-aged families with kids, older empty nesters, or singles in their twenties and thirties. A check of the homeownership rate can tell you whether it's the type of place where people plant long-term roots, or if there's a thriving rental market that could support your home as an investment purchase.

Trulia, Niche, NeighborhoodScout, GreatSchools, SpotCrime, and Other Websites

There's a whole cottage industry of community comparison websites that put that census data into greater context, while also parsing publicly available data on everything from local schools to crime statistics.

The free real estate website Trulia.com is particularly useful in this regard, thanks to its What Locals Say feature, which invites local users to answer questions about their own neighborhoods. The answers should be taken with a grain of salt, but this feature does offer a unique window into the personality of a place. You can see how many locals agree that their neighbors decorate for holidays, for example, or whether they feel safe walking around at night or tend to see kids playing outside or people walking dogs.

Crime-mapping sites such as SpotCrime.com display recent police activity with at-a-glance icons that differentiate between minor infractions and more serious crimes. Incidents of petty theft or vandalism may not be a concern to you, but a cluster of assaults or armed robberies probably would be. The nonprofit GreatSchools.org, meanwhile, offers an independent source of school ratings that go beyond just test scores to measure equity, student progress, and college readiness.

Walk This Way

If car-free means care-free to you, check a neighborhood's walkability rating, bike friendliness, and public transit accessibility on WalkScore.com. A Walk Score of 70 or higher is considered very walkable, meaning most errands can be accomplished on foot.

Air Quality Index

More and more research has shown that local air quality can impact everything from long-term health to short-term cognitive function. For example, children and adults alike perform worse on cognitive tests when there are higher levels of particulate matter in the air. And people exposed to more air pollution have a greater risk of developing both acute health problems (for example, an asthma attack) and long-term health conditions.

Sites like BreezoMeter.com allow you to view air quality heat maps in a given area, where you can clearly see persistent pockets of particulate matter and ozone in certain areas, such as those near a highway or industrial zone.

FEMA Flood Maps

Before you fall head over heels for a place, make sure it will still be there thirty years from now. As sea levels rise and climate change brings increased risk of flooding along coasts and inland waterways, it's more important than ever to consider an area's flood risk.

You can view current flood maps from the Federal Emergency Management Agency (FEMA) at www.fema.gov/flood-maps to determine whether homes in a certain area will require flood insurance or are at greater risk of flooding during a bad storm. These maps can also help you find the relative high ground in a given neighborhood.

Even if many of the homes are at risk of flooding, that doesn't have to preclude a neighborhood from consideration. But it may mean you'll want to look at homes that are flood resilient—with any essential home systems elevated above the floodplain, for example.

Property Tax Rates

Local real estate taxes can vary quite substantially, even among neighboring communities. A quick Internet search can generally provide you with the property tax rate of a community you're interested in. These are usually expressed as dollars per $1,000 of assessed value. A property tax rate of $12.30 per $1,000, for example, essentially translates to a rate of 1.23 percent of the home's assessed value. Check out the town's website to see what services that includes, such as curbside trash pickup, and whether there are any additional school or transit taxes.

Election Results

Depending on how political you are and whether you'd prefer to be in the company of like-minded neighbors, you may want to review past election results and turnout figures to glean some clues to a community's collective priorities. Look at the results from both national and local races—the combination can paint a more complete and nuanced picture of the electorate.

Sex Offender Registries

Some states require convicted sex offenders to register their home addresses, which are then maintained in a public database. Before moving into a neighborhood, a cursory check of the registry may be worth it, particularly if you have kids.

Youth Programs and School Lunch Menus

Even if you don't have a school-aged child, the services a community provides to its kids can tell you a lot about the place and the people who live there. It can be a real pain navigating a clunky municipal website, but see if the town's school lunch menus are published online. (If they're not, that alone says something about the place.)

Is it a lot of pizza and potatoes, or are there plenty of healthy, multicultural, or vegetarian options too? The latter may indicate a school district that serves a more forward-thinking community; some schools even partner with local organic farms and butchers.

Meanwhile, research what kind of youth sports, summer camps, and enrichment programs are available to local kids. Are there a lot of options—everything from Little League to LEGO Camp? Are they free or subsidized? Some cities devote tremendous resources to kids' programming, offering everything from sailing lessons to free art camps staffed by local teens.

LOCK IN YOUR TARGET(S)

Your search doesn't need to culminate in one specific target neighborhood, but that can be very helpful, since you can focus all of your energy on one square mile or so and work with a Realtor who has deep ties to that community. But you should be able to boil things down to a few finalists at most—at which point, it's time to start your house hunt in earnest.

Chapter 7

The House Hunt

Now that you've narrowed down your "where," it's time to think about the "what"—what kind of home do you want? Are you thinking about new construction, or do you crave the quirky charm of an older home? Could you live with a fixer-upper? Would you consider a condo—or even a money-making multifamily? When you imagine your home, what does it look like, and what does it absolutely need to have to meet your expectations?

In this chapter, you'll learn about different home types, including condos and new construction, and how to prioritize your needs and wants (and which of those wants can be addressed later). Then we'll get you ready to put this knowledge into practice with tips for scouring home listings online and for touring homes with a keen eye for what matters—without getting too distracted by fun, shiny things.

DETERMINE YOUR MUST-HAVES VERSUS NICE-TO-HAVES

Getting Your Priorities Straight

There are things you want in a home, and things you absolutely need it to have. It's time to parse the difference into a needs and wants list.

This shouldn't come as a surprise, but unless you have gobs and gobs of money, you're probably going to have to make some trade-offs to find the right home within your budget. As a first-time buyer, success means finding a place that meets your most urgent needs and, if you're lucky, maybe even fulfills many of your wish-list desires as well. But in all likelihood, something on that "wants" list will have to go.

It's crucial to have a clear-eyed understanding of what you absolutely cannot compromise on, and what home features you would really love to have—but could, if necessary, live without, at least for the time being. And it's important to communicate this information to your real estate agent, who can keep those criteria in mind while scouting new listings on your behalf.

What's more, if you're house hunting with a partner, now is the time to get on the same page—or at least develop a combined list of must-haves. You may discover you have very different priorities, depending on which chores each of you normally handles, or competing ideas of what a home ought to look or feel like.

Be honest about what matters most to you, thoughtful about what you could live without, and sensitive to each other's expectations—this is your partner's dream too. If there's not a lot of common ground, and your lists of necessities begin to bloat, you may each need to whittle down your wishes to a handful of must-haves.

NEED, REALLY WANT, NICE-TO-HAVE, OR DON'T CARE?

Beyond identifying your most essential needs, you also want to prioritize your preferences by ranking your wish-list features—we'll call them really-wants and nice-to-haves. Then there are home features you could take or leave—the don't-care items.

You can start making this list as soon as you have an idea of "home" in your head. But keep adding to it and refining it. The list may evolve over time as you tour more homes and start to get a better sense of what's available in your price range. Keep your Realtor informed of any changes if your priorities shift. Anytime you can kick an item further down the list—bumping a need down to a really-want, for example, or a really-want down to a nice-to-have—it will make your home search easier and, in all likelihood, less expensive.

Needs

Ask yourself: What are some of the things a home absolutely *must* have if you're going to spend hundreds of thousands of dollars on it and live there for at least the next few years of your life? What are the deal breakers that you simply can't live without?

This list will be different for everyone, depending on your lifestyle and future plans, but it boils down to your most basic demands. The bottom line is this: *If you can't buy a home that has these features, then you'd just as soon rent a place that does and not buy a home at all.*

For example, you would probably love a home with a stylish, remodeled kitchen plucked from the pages of an interior design magazine. Is that a must-have? Likely not. But a dishwasher? That might be a must-have. Ditto an eat-in kitchen.

Here are some examples of needs or must-haves:

- Work from home? You might view an office—or at least some kind of workspace, such as an upstairs landing with room for a desk—as essential.
- Have kids, or plan to? Maybe three bedrooms is the absolute minimum you'd consider. If you have a toddler, a bathtub may be mandatory; a family with teens, meanwhile, may insist on having at least two bathrooms.
- Got a dog? You may limit your search to homes with fenced-in yards, and condo buyers will need to look exclusively at pet-friendly buildings.
- Do you have aging parents or close family members who visit from out of state? Maybe you need a guest space with its own bath.
- Are you an artist or woodworker? Perhaps you need some kind of space—whether it's a garage, shed, attic, or basement—for a studio or workshop.
- After living in a downtown apartment and battling for street parking every day, maybe a driveway or dedicated garage spot is at the top of your must-have list.
- Having spent months trapped at home during COVID lockdowns, perhaps you're now unwilling to consider a home without some kind of private outdoor space—whether it's a yard, patio, or porch.

Putting a Price on Potential

Sometimes a must-have includes the potential to meet the need: Even if the yard isn't fenced in right now, for example, could it be fenced in later on? In that case, you may lower what you'd be willing to pay for the home by the cost of installing a new fence, but you don't need to cross it off your list entirely.

Really-Wants

While your needs list can help you eliminate homes from consideration, your really-wants are the things that elevate a home's value in your eyes. These are the features and flourishes that would bring you great joy and that you would probably be willing to stretch your budget to get.

Some big wants may include a fireplace or woodstove for cozy winter nights, a big backyard with room for a garden, a laundry room, or a home that doesn't need significant remodeling or repairs.

Maybe you've always dreamed of a sunny great room with cathedral ceilings and skylights, or a farmer's porch out front. What are the things that would make you actually fall in love with a place?

Nice-to-Haves

There are lots of home features you may consider to be a nice perk, but nowhere near necessary. These are lower-priority wants, but ones that could nonetheless tip the scales in favor of one home over another.

An example: You *need* a garage, you *really want* it to be attached to the home, and it would be *nice to have* a two-car garage with automatic door openers and a loft for extra storage.

Don't-Cares

Finally, there's the "don't care" list. These are home features that some buyers seek out but that don't really matter to you. For example, if you and your partner both work remotely, you may not care whether a home is close to a subway or train station.

Why make a category for stuff you don't care about? Because this is your competitive advantage over other buyers. To use the garage example again: If you don't really care about having a garage, you can shop for homes without one, and you won't face as much competition from the many buyers who view that feature as essential.

SINGLE-FAMILY, CONDO, OR MULTIFAMILY?

The Pros and Cons of Each

Homes come in all shapes, sizes, and conditions. But one home feature makes a particularly big difference: whether it's a single-family house, condominium, or multifamily home.

You may have your heart set on a single-family house—maybe it's even on your must-have list—or you may be open to whatever property can cross off all of your needs and get you into the neighborhood you love at the right price. Keeping your mind open can make your home search easier, as you'll have more options to choose from (and you may be surprised by how houselike some condos can feel). But either way, it's helpful to know the benefits and drawbacks of each property type.

SINGLE-FAMILY HOUSES

A single-family house is the most common type of residential property in the United States. About two-thirds of all housing units (67 percent) are single-family homes, according to census data. It's also the housing type that most home buyers say they would prefer, if price wasn't a concern. (But, of course, it is.) Here are some of the pros and cons to buying a traditional house:

Pros
- Purchasing a single-family home means you also own the land beneath it, which puts you in complete control of your property.

(At least, to the extent your community allows—you would likely need to apply for a zoning variance if you wanted to convert your home into a hotel, for example, or build a helipad in your front yard.)

- A detached, single-family home will generally offer the most privacy from neighbors. Even if the home is on a small lot in a dense neighborhood, you won't have anyone stomping around above, beneath, or beside you. You'll generally have at least some kind of yard or outdoor space to call your own—and since you own the lot, you can put up a fence or plant a hedgerow for added privacy.
- As the predominant housing type in America, single-family homes can be a somewhat more reliable investment than other types of property. They held their value better than condos during the Great Recession, according to a Redfin analysis.

Cons

- Single-family homes are generally more expensive than condos, all else being equal.
- As discussed in Chapter 1, owning a home can be an expensive and time-consuming responsibility; owning a single-family home means all of that falls squarely upon you. There's no one else with whom to share the costs or burdens of homeownership and maintenance.

CONDOMINIUMS

A condominium is one piece of a larger property. When you buy a condo, you're getting exclusive ownership of the cubic feet of interior airspace within your unit, plus a proportional common interest in the rest of the building—including the walls, roof, and the land it sits on. That creates some interesting pros and cons.

Pros

- Since you're only buying a piece of a property (and a diluted share of the land it sits on), and sharing many maintenance expenses with other owners, condos are generally the lowest-cost way to achieve homeownership.

- Condos can offer a less intense introduction to homeownership. You may have to deal with a few homeowner headaches, like replacing your hot water heater or remodeling a bathroom. But much of the routine maintenance (such as exterior painting, landscaping, and snow removal) may be included in your association fee, and major expenses (such as roof replacement) are typically shared by the entire complex.

- A condo building can offer perks and amenities you may not be able to find (or want to deal with) in a single-family home, such as a health club or pool.

- Condos come in all settings and styles, not just high-rise buildings. Townhouses are essentially condos, except that they have a private entrance and often live more like a single-family home, with two or more floors of living space. You can find condos in converted Victorians or standalone cottages that share property management costs.

Cons

- Shared ownership comes with less privacy and control, and more rules and regulations. You may not be able to have certain types of pets, for example, or rent out your unit as a vacation rental; in some buildings, you could even be fined for making too much noise. (We'll discuss condo rules and regulations in more detail in the next section.)

- You may have to negotiate with other owners when it comes to funding improvements or seeking approval for a remodeling project in your unit.
- While condo fees often cover expenses you'd have to pay anyway—such as water and real estate taxes—sometimes they include more luxurious amenities than you need. Twenty-four-hour concierge service or valet parking can be a nice perk, but that portion of your mortgage payment is a fixed ownership cost that isn't building you any equity. That can suppress resale values in condo complexes with high fees.
- If a condo association doesn't have enough money in reserves (excess savings held in an escrow account), owners may be charged a "special assessment" to finance urgent repairs or big improvements, such as a new roof deck or laundry facility. Even if you can't afford a $5,000 one-time payment to help pay for a new parking area, for example, you may be on the hook for it if enough of the other owners vote in favor of the measure.
- Some mortgages have stricter rules about purchasing a condo. For example, FHA loans can't be used to finance a condo if the building is less than half owner-occupied, isn't yet completed, or doesn't keep at least 10 percent of its HOA budget in reserves.

The Worst of Both Worlds?

Some single-family homes in planned developments or gated communities are also part of a homeowners' association (HOA), which typically means owners must pay HOA fees. These fees can be modest, and may be used to maintain perks like tennis courts or a pool. But HOAs can also impose strict rules on homeowners, limiting the freedom of single-family homeownership. For example, you may have to ask permission before painting your home a different color, or you could incur fines for an untidy yard or leaving up holiday decorations for too long.

MULTIFAMILY HOUSES

Multifamily homes are residential properties with two to four units. Whether it's a side-by-side duplex, a New England–style triple-decker, a postwar brick fourplex, or an old Victorian carved up into separate apartments, buying a multifamily home to live in while renting out the other units has long been a gateway to real estate investment. It's not without its challenges, however.

Pros

- If you're able to live in a multifamily home and rent out the other unit(s), someone else is essentially paying part of your mortgage. While your mortgage payment will remain fixed, rents generally rise over time along with inflation (and often even faster than that). At some point, rent from your tenants may cover your entire mortgage.
- Most lenders will allow you to count a portion of the estimated rent toward your income for mortgage qualification purchases, meaning you can qualify for a bigger loan when purchasing a multifamily property.
- A *multifamily* home is also great for *one* family: If you have aging parents, adult children, visiting relatives, or other family members you'd like to have nearby, you can invite them to live with you while still enjoying some privacy.

Cons

- Owning a two- or three-family house means two or three times the headaches. Lots of things inevitably break in a typical home, from the water heater to the furnace to the refrigerator; you'll now own two or three of all of them!

- It's not easy being a landlord. The job comes with a lot of responsibilities, not to mention that you'll need to be mindful of fair housing laws. You may luck out and get respectful tenants who never miss a rent check, but you could also end up with rowdy renters who rarely pay on time. And even the best tenants may need to call you in the middle of the night or during a holiday weekend because the heat stopped working or their kitchen sink is leaking—and it's on you to get it fixed.

- It's a different dynamic from living in a condo building, because you're the only owner—but the fact remains that you'll be living in closer quarters with your neighbors than if you were to own a single-family house.

UNDERSTANDING CONDO DOCUMENTS AND BYLAWS

What Are You Buying Into?

When you purchase a condo, you're buying more than just a single unit within a larger complex. You're also entering into a binding financial and social contract with the other owners; your fates and fortunes will soon be intertwined. So before you purchase a condo, you need to review the association's bylaws, budget, and other documents to know what you're getting yourself into.

In some states, buyers have a legal right to review condo documents for a set number of days before proceeding with a purchase; the seller must provide copies of key condo documents. Elsewhere, it's common for condo buyers to make their offer subject to a review of the association documents and budget. If the buyer (or the buyer's attorney) sees anything amiss, they can pull out of the purchase.

WHAT ARE CONDO DOCUMENTS?

What exactly is in those documents? You may find an overwhelming amount of information in hundreds of pages of boring and confusing legal language. In fact, it's well worth having a real estate attorney review the documents for you. But these documents will answer some important questions about the building or complex you're looking at, how it's managed, and what you can expect as an owner. The particulars vary by state, but here are some key things to look for in the condo documents.

Covenants, Conditions, and Restrictions (CC&Rs)

Every condo association has some sort of formal declaration or master deed that is recorded with the state. This legally defines the development and the physical spaces within it, as well as various owner obligations and property use restrictions.

Often called the declaration of covenants, conditions, and restrictions (CC&Rs), this document will map out the location and measurements of each unit, define common areas, and spell out the rights and responsibilities of individual owners—as well as the authority of the association to enforce rules and collect dues.

This is where you'll find high-level information about what you can and cannot do as an owner. For example, CC&Rs may detail:

- Whether the association has an age restriction
- How condo fees are calculated and collected
- Whether pets are allowed, and if any types, sizes, or breeds are excluded
- What's expected of owners in terms of maintenance
- Whether owners are allowed to rent out their units
- Whether vacation rentals (such as Airbnb or Vrbo) are permitted
- What the enforcement policies or penalties are for owners who break the rules

Bylaws

A condo association's bylaws outline how the association is run. For example, the bylaws may spell out how often meetings are held and when and how voting should be conducted. If there's a board of directors or trustees, the bylaws will outline how many people serve on the board, for how long, and how they're chosen. Bylaws may also explain the process for collecting fees and for setting the budget along with other procedural instructions.

Rules and Regulations

Not every rule is important enough or permanent enough to make it into the official CC&Rs. New and sometimes very specific rules come and go as warranted or voted upon, and those accumulate under a separate set of rules and regulations.

These rules can range from the obvious (pick up after your dog) to the more arbitrary (no kids in the pool after 8 p.m.) to the nitty-gritty (no fence shall be higher than 4 feet 11 inches). Nonetheless, they are still the law of the land, unless the association votes to change them.

Financial Reserves

How much money does the association currently have in reserves? Especially if it's an older property, consider whether there's enough cash in reserves to cover the cost of a major repair, such as replacing the building's roof or rebuilding the decks. If the reserves are nearly drained, and a major maintenance project comes up, you and the other owners could be hit with a special assessment—an extra one-time fee to cover the cost of the work.

Operating Budget

A quick peek at the condo association's monthly budget can tell you where and how your fees will be spent. Do the expenses appear to be organized and well managed? Do any charges look oddly high, inconsistent, or unnecessary? Is the association setting aside at least 10 percent to 15 percent of its budget into its reserve fund each month?

Meeting Minutes

Sellers aren't always able or required to provide the minutes from recent association meetings, but it's good to ask for them. Review the notes from recent meetings to see what topics seem to dominate the discussions, whether owners appear to be in agreement or in a state of discord, and if there are any big (and expensive) projects being floated.

Questions to Ask

In addition to reviewing the condo documents, ask the seller:

- How many of the units are owner-occupied, and how many are rented to tenants? Have there been any recent foreclosures or vacancies?
- Are there any upcoming projects or improvements planned? How much are they slated to cost, and where will the money come from?
- Have there been any special assessments in the past year?
- Are there any current lawsuits or liens against the association?

NEW CONSTRUCTION VERSUS EXISTING HOMES

What to Know When Buying New

Most home buyers end up purchasing an existing home, whether it was built two decades ago or two centuries ago; in fact, only about 13 percent of all home sales in 2020 were newly built homes. However, almost half (43 percent) of those new homes were sold to first-time buyers, according to the National Association of Home Builders.

There's a lot to be said for buying or building a brand-new home, including the fact that you can often get exactly what you're looking for, down to the paint, flooring, and finishes. But it can add some complications and costs to your home search as well.

PROS OF NEW CONSTRUCTION

- **A brand-new home:** There's an undeniable appeal to living in a home that has never had another owner, where every surface is sparkling clean. And although home systems like furnaces and roofs have a limited life cycle (which you'll learn about later in this chapter), in a new home, you can expect clear sailing for the first five to ten years, and many builders offer a limited warranty in case anything breaks.
- **Safe, energy-efficient construction:** New homes are built to modern safety and efficiency standards, so you'll have an easier (and cheaper) time heating and cooling your home. You won't have to worry about outdated electrical wiring, rusty old pipes, or

once-common but harmful construction materials like lead paint or asbestos.

- **Customizable options:** If you purchase a new home before it's completed, you can typically add custom upgrades or even choose from a few different floor plans. These add-ons can take the cost well above the base price, so try not to get carried away.
- **Modern floor plans:** Most new homes have more modern layouts, with open-concept kitchens and larger rooms, doorways, and closets than you may find in an older house.
- **Amenities:** Some larger new developments include common spaces, like a clubhouse, tennis courts, or pool. New condo developments in the city might include a shared roof deck or health club.

CONS OF NEW CONSTRUCTION

- **Price:** Newly built homes will generally cost more than existing homes. Some of this price premium—but not all of it—can be offset by maintenance savings, since you shouldn't have any big projects to deal with early on.
- **Location:** New construction developments often pop up on the outskirts of a metro area, where land is cheapest. Even if the commute isn't too bad (or is a nonissue), there may not be much of interest nearby, and the site itself may not have any mature trees.
- **Timeline:** If you're custom-building a home or buying into a development before it's finished, it will be many months before you can move into your new home—and there may be construction delays along the way.
- **Environment:** Buying or remodeling an existing home is generally more eco-friendly than building a new one from scratch.

While a new home will be more efficient, it can take decades for those energy savings to offset the carbon footprint of brand-new construction.

- **Uniformity:** As much as you can customize a new build in progress, homes in a new development are typically pretty similar to each other—variations on a theme at best. That can make it hard for your home to stand out when it comes time to sell: If your neighbor's home is roughly the same size, shape, and layout, then whoever prices their home lowest will sell first. (This isn't an issue for custom-built homes on a private lot.)

BUYING A NEW HOME

The purchase process for new construction is similar to buying an existing home, but there are some important differences to keep in mind.

New Home Shopping

Whether you're buying a home in a new development or hiring a custom builder to construct your dream home, it's important to research and vet the homebuilder. Read online reviews and make sure the builder appears to be financially stable (and not about to declare bankruptcy with your deposit check in hand). Check out the builder's portfolio of previous developments—including an in-person visit—and even talk to owners there if possible. Have their homes held up well? If they had any issues, did the builder address them promptly and fairly?

Often, buying a new home is a little more like a typical retail purchase, like buying a house at the mall. But you should still work with a buyer's agent and bring them with you when you first tour the model home or construction site, so the builder's agent or sales team can't claim to be your (very compromised) buyer's agent.

While the sticker price of a new home is typically set in granite, other costs like custom upgrades and premium finishes may be more negotiable. A buyer's agent who's experienced with new construction can help you pick your battles—and counsel you on which upgrades may be worth it when it comes to resale value, and which ones aren't. Your buyer's agent will also be able to review and explain the sales contract, including the deposit schedule, construction timeline, and what recourse you have if the home isn't completed on time or as agreed.

The Model Home Menu

While a model home is an indication of what the builder is *capable* of creating, remember that it's probably outfitted with premium upgrades; the bonus sunroom and chef's kitchen package might add another $80,000 to the base price. Ask for a list of exactly what is included in the base package, which features are considered upgrades, and how much each one costs.

Financing a New Home

If you're building a custom home, or buying into a development during the construction phase (as opposed to an already completed home), you'll need a different type of mortgage since there isn't yet a home for the lender to appraise and accept as collateral. Here are your options:

- A construction loan is a short-term, higher-interest loan you can use to finance the cost of land and to pay incremental installments to the builder as construction reaches certain milestones. Once the home is complete, you pay off that loan with a separate, standard mortgage—which means you'll pay two sets of closing costs.

- A construction-to-permanent loan is a hybrid mortgage that begins as a construction loan and then converts to a standard, fixed-rate mortgage once the home is finished. The big benefit is that you'll only pay one set of closing costs. Not all lenders offer this type of loan, though, and it can be more expensive than a traditional mortgage—for example, you may need to lock in your interest rate not just for sixty days but for six or nine months.

- Some builders have their own preferred lender who will offer these financing options; they may even require or pressure you to work with them. If there are no fees attached, it's usually fine to get preapproved by the developer's lender, but keep in mind that you'll usually still be free to shop around for the best mortgage.

HOW TO SEARCH WITH INTENT—AND INTENSITY

Setting New Listing Alerts, Finding Off-Market Listings, and Other House Hunting Tips

You've determined what kind of home you want—now it's time to find it. Your agent can and should help in this pursuit, suggesting homes for sale that fit your criteria. But you can take an active role in your home search as well and alert your agent to listings you want to tour.

Where to Find Homes for Sale

Twenty years ago, real estate agents were the gatekeepers of all home listings; it was hard for buyers to do their own house hunting without access to the local MLS (Multiple Listing Service) database. Now that information is publicly available online—and virtually every home for sale, all over the country (and even the world), is at your fingertips.

So how do you find your first home among the many thousands for sale? If you haven't already, start browsing homes for sale on one or more of the major real estate websites. Zillow.com, Trulia.com, Redfin.com, and Realtor.com all make house hunting easy.

All of these sites offer ways to filter and refine your search—by price, neighborhood, square footage, number of bedrooms, home features, and specific keywords—which will be a critical resource for you. And each site has its pros and cons. *Zillow* includes rentals as well as homes for sale, but its interface can be a little clunky. *Trulia* provides a treasure trove of neighborhood information. *Redfin* offers an intuitive user experience and some of the most granular filtering options—and unlike the other sites, it's also a brokerage, so it may include some forthcoming listings you won't see elsewhere. However, *Redfin* isn't available in all markets.

Set up a free account with each site—and download the apps to your phone, too, since you'll be checking homes often and on the fly—and see which platform you like the best. That will become your go-to home search engine. Most allow you to save your favorite listings and share them with a partner.

The Deal with Discount Brokerages

Some brokerages, notably Redfin at the national level, offer discounted agent commissions or even a rebate to buyers who use them. There's no question that the real estate business model is ripe for disruption, and technology has successfully subsumed many of the services agents used to provide.

But since buyers don't pay their agents directly, lower commissions are a bigger perk to a seller than to a buyer. Agents at discount brokerages can often be spread too thin to provide the kind of ultra-attentive service a first-time buyer needs. So experts recommend working with an experienced buyer's agent who's fully dedicated to your home search.

Using Search Filters

Search filters are an essential tool to help you find the proverbial needle that is your dream home within the haystack of the housing market. Enter your needs, some of your biggest wants, and your price limit, and *voilà*! You'll instantly see which listings match your criteria. But it's worth tweaking your filters to see what comes up in different searches too.

For example, you probably have a sweet spot in your price range—let's say it's $300,000 to $400,000. But you should open up your search a bit wider than that: You may still be able to afford a home priced at $409,000, if the seller is willing to entertain below-asking-price offers.

Search filters are your friend, but they can sometimes be your foe too. If a Realtor doesn't input the listing correctly, a worthwhile home may escape your search. Other times, a home might offer what you're looking for, but only if you use a bit of imagination or connect a couple of dots.

If you're looking exclusively at three-bedroom homes because you need a guest room for visiting family, for example, you may miss out on a two-bedroom house with a separate guest studio, or an office that could easily be converted to a spare bedroom.

It's also worth searching for variations on important keywords. For example, if you're specifically searching for a "waterfront" home and a Realtor describes a waterfront home as "lakefront," the listing may not appear in your searches. Ditto if the listing agent misspells a crucial adjective or school name. So every once in a while, make it a point to look beyond the filters.

Setting Up New Listing Alerts

Once you've settled on a search platform you like, you might want to set up a couple of new listing alerts, so you can learn about new homes hitting the market. Start by signing up for a daily alert that notifies you of any new listings within your price and geographic range—for example, any home between $300,000 and $425,000 in the community you're targeting.

You may want to add an immediate alert anytime a home hits the market that fits your more precise criteria. For example, you could get an instant alert whenever a home in that price range is listed with three bedrooms, two or more bathrooms, plus a garage, fireplace, and pool.

Finally, keep an eye on the broader market. It's worthwhile to get a weekly update of every home for sale in the community or neighborhood you're interested in. That will help you gain a better understanding of local pricing trends and keep you from missing out on a quirky listing that falls through the search-filter cracks.

If all those alerts leave you feeling overwhelmed, you can always dial back the frequency, or simply rely on your own daily check-ins. (*Redfin* even offers a constantly updated, scrollable news-feed-style algorithm of new listings you might like, based on the homes you've already saved as "favorites.")

Off- and Pre-Market Listings

Not every home for sale makes it to the MLS. How do you learn about them? Some real estate agents, particularly those at big brokerages or those who are well connected in the community, hear about new listings before they hit the market. This can give you a slight edge as a buyer, especially in a competitive market.

If your Realtor's colleague has a new listing, for example, and offers a preview to other agents in the office, your agent may be able to place an offer for you before the home ever reaches the MLS. This is called a pocket listing, and it's generally not a great deal for the seller, who normally would want as many buyers as possible to see and bid on their home, driving up the price. However, if a seller was hoping to get $350,000 for their home, and you're willing to pay $375,000 before it even goes to market, then they may agree to just take the deal in hand. (The one big concern here is the potential conflict of interest it creates if your buyer's agent and the listing agent work for the same brokerage; your agent could face pressure to close the deal.)

Your agent isn't the only one who can find upcoming listings, though. Keep your eyes and ears open. Check community *Facebook* groups and online discussion boards, and talk to people at playgrounds and coffee shops to see if anyone knows a neighbor preparing to sell. Check local classified ads and FSBO.com for homes being sold by the owner.

If you have your heart set on a particular neighborhood, drive around looking for signs of potential turnover: A dumpster in the driveway may simply indicate a remodeling project underway...but it could also signal a clean-out in advance of an upcoming sale. Ask your Realtor to keep it on their radar.

WHY YOU SHOULD TOUR FIFTY HOMES

That's Not As Crazy As It Sounds

As you find promising listings, it's time to start touring them with your buyer's agent. Find your most comfortable shoes, because this may take a while.

Watching a show like *House Hunters* on HGTV—where buyers tour just three homes for sale, one of which is almost always over budget, and then choose one to purchase—you may think the home search process could be tidily wrapped up in a weekend. But that's not usually how it works in real life. (And by some accounts, it's not how it works for TV buyers, either.) The average American home buyer reported touring nine homes over the course of an eight-week home search in 2020, according to the National Association of Realtors.

When it comes to home tours, more is better. Touring homes for sale isn't just about finding a home to buy—it's one of the most important parts of your home buying education.

Every home you enter, every yard you walk through, every countertop you run your hand over—whether it makes your eyes bulge with envy or your nose crinkle in disapproval—provides you with more information about what features you value the most and what it costs to get them within the reality of your local housing market.

Some buyers do fall in love with the first or second home they see and are lucky enough to get an offer accepted right away. Most others, though, will spend weeks or even months homing in on the right choice. That's time well spent: Each home you see will make you a more informed buyer. But still...fifty homes? Really? Well, yes—and no.

HOW TO TOUR HOMES

There may not even be fifty homes for sale in the community you're targeting. However, if you accept that a "home tour" doesn't have to be a formal real estate showing with your Realtor present, and if you start early, you can tour a lot more homes than you think.

Open Houses

Once you've decided that you'd like to buy a home, even if you're not yet financially prepared, start popping into open houses. They don't have to be homes that you would consider buying, or even homes you can afford—at this point, it's just field research. Take note of the price, size, location, and condition of the home, and whether that combination has resulted in a big, eager crowd of hopeful buyers...or a quiet, nearly empty house.

Dinner Parties

Every home you step foot in from now on should be considered a "home tour." Visiting your in-laws, or stopping by a friend's party? Time to tune your senses in to things you might have overlooked in the past: Pay closer attention to details like the floor plan and finishes, and make mental notes of qualities you like or don't.

Ask these homeowners where they got the fixtures you like, or how well their new flooring has held up. Find out whether they like living with the features you admire, or if there are actually frustrating downsides to them. For example, rustic, rolling barn doors can be a stylish and space-saving way to close off a closet or powder room, but some homeowners find that they jam easily or fall off their track, making them less glamorous in everyday life.

Online Tours

Increasingly, home sellers are relying on virtual showings. Wherever possible, this is something you should take advantage of.

An online 3-D tour is a great way to explore a home from afar, and it can tell you a lot about its layout, light, and functionality. It can help you rule out homes that look appealing in well-staged photos but fail the "flow test" on a virtual walk-through—once you discover, for example, that the glamorously updated bathroom pictured in the listing is actually down a steep basement stairway, not off the upstairs bedrooms as you had imagined.

However, a virtual visit is usually a poor substitute for the full-sensory experience of visiting a home in person. You won't hear the squeak of loose floorboards in a virtual tour, for example, or the rumble of trucks passing by on a busy road. You probably won't notice the crumbling grout in the corner of the bathroom or be able to tell the difference between laminate and hardwood flooring. It's impossible to detect a lingering odor of tobacco or musty mildew. And you won't be able to get a literal feel for the texture of the countertops, cabinets, and other surfaces, or the tug of a sticky closet door that's a struggle to open.

So the best use of virtual tours is as a way to screen new listings—to determine which ones are worth the effort of an in-person visit and which ones you can skip.

Send Your Realtor

Another way to make your home search more efficient is to let your real estate agent filter listings for you. Realtors often get a first look at new homes as they hit the market. If you've been working together for a while and communicating your tastes and preferences, your Realtor will be able to tell you if a new listing is worth your time or one you can safely ignore, and why.

And if you can't see a home in person—if you're relocating from another area, for example, or simply crunched for time—your real estate agent may be able to tour the place for you using FaceTime or another video calling service. In addition to getting your Realtor's expert opinion, that will allow you to ask questions in real time and zoom in on things you'd like a closer look at.

Have Someone Take a Tour

If you make an offer remotely, make sure your Realtor has toured the property on your behalf and that you trust their judgment. You can (and should) also try to see the home in person before you finalize the sale—during the home inspection, for example.

Beware of Buyer's Blur

All that said, touring too many homes in short succession can create a whirlwind sensation—before long, you can't remember which house had the creepy basement and which one had the creepy neighbor.

Once you're in the heat of your home search, use the aforementioned strategies to try to limit the number of homes you formally tour to two or three serious contenders per week. Take lots of photos with your cell phone to remind yourself later of little details or issues that catch your eye. It can even be helpful to jot down some quick thoughts or record your first impressions in a short voice memo to yourself once you're back in the car.

UNDERSTANDING MAJOR HOME SYSTEMS

A Crash Course in Building Biology

Buildings have their own kind of biology, a core set of systems that help them function properly. You can think of the framing and structure of a building as its skeleton, for example, and the roof, siding, and windows as its skin. The heating, cooling, and plumbing systems, meanwhile, are essentially the building's circulatory system; the wiring, its nervous system.

The condition of a home's major mechanical systems can tell you a lot about the building's health and what it will be like to live in it, so here are some things to look for as you tour a home.

Heating and Cooling

Heating, ventilation, and air conditioning (HVAC) account for about half of all the energy used in a typical American home, according to the US Department of Energy. But these systems don't just impact your utility bills—they also determine your day-to-day comfort.

There are various ways to condition the air inside your home, and the systems tasked with this job will vary by region. In the Northeast and Midwest, for example, heating is a more crucial concern than air conditioning, while the opposite is often true in the Southwest.

If you compare a home's heating system to the body's circulatory system, there are two traditional types of "hearts"—furnaces and boilers—and two styles of "arteries" by which heat gets delivered:

- **Furnace and forced air:** A furnace heats up air and blows that hot air through a system of air ducts—those boxy, silvery tunnels that spies always seem to be crawling through in the movies—which deliver the warm air into the living space through vents. A forced hot air system can start delivering heat to a room almost instantly, and the ductwork makes installing central air easier. However, those ducts can leak air and lose efficiency, and the blowing air can be bothersome for people with allergies.
- **Boiler and radiators:** A boiler heats up water and pushes either hot water or even hotter steam through a system of pipes to baseboard or floor-standing radiators in the living space. Radiators take a while to warm up, but once hot (and be careful, as some can get very hot), they gently radiate heat into the room for quite a while. While it's an efficient heating method, sending hot water or steam through metal pipes brings the potential for water leaks.

Newer heating technologies include radiant floor heat and heat pumps. Radiant heat relies on heated coils beneath the floor, which warm the surface and, in turn, the room above. Hydronic floor heat—where the coils are filled with liquid, heated by a boiler—is efficient and cost-effective; electric coils are costlier to heat with, but are a good option for a bathroom or addition.

Heat pumps are a highly efficient source of electric heat; they're essentially air conditioners that run in reverse. There is always some amount of heat energy in the outside air, even on a very cold day, and heat pumps grab that warmth, condense it, and bring it inside. They can also operate in cooling mode during the summer, making them a go-to HVAC solution.

Heat pumps can supplement or even replace a forced hot air system, providing heating and cooling through the existing air ducts. They can also be broken up into "ductless mini-split" systems for boiler-heated homes without ductwork—where a main heat pump outside powers a handful of blower units in different rooms of the home.

When touring a home, try out the heating and cooling systems to see how well they perform and how noisy they are. In the world of HVAC, newer is almost always better. An old boiler could run for decades, but even if it's still kicking, it's probably very inefficient compared to newer models. Replacing a furnace or boiler will generally cost a few thousand dollars or more.

HVAC equipment needs regular maintenance, such as changing air filters. If well maintained, a new furnace or gas boiler ought to last up to twenty years, according to a study by the National Association of Home Builders. A heat pump ought to last sixteen years, and a new central air conditioning unit should work well for ten to fifteen years.

How Old Is It in Roof Years?

Some things in your home can last forever; others will almost certainly need to be replaced. Here are the average lifespans of common home systems and building materials, according to a study by the National Association of Home Builders:

- Gas or electric water heater: 10 years
- Tankless water heater: 20 years
- Faucets: 15–20 years
- Furnace: 15–20 years
- Boiler: 13–21 years
- Asphalt roof: 20 years
- Slate or copper roof: 50 years
- Refrigerators: 13 years
- Dishwashers: 9 years

Plumbing

Your first impression of a home's plumbing will be the shiny faucets, and of course you'll want to test the function and water pressure of these fixtures. But the guts beneath the sink and behind the walls are far more important.

You can't see through walls, but check the condition of any visible pipes under sinks and in the basement, and look for signs of past leaks—discolored areas on the ceilings, beams, or floors. Make sure all sinks, toilets, and appliances have shut-off valves nearby, where you could stop the water flow locally in the event of a leak or to perform simple maintenance.

Whether powered by gas, electricity, or solar power, there are two types of hot water heaters: traditional and tankless (or on-demand). A traditional hot water heater keeps a large tank of hot water at the ready—typically forty to fifty gallons, or enough for a couple of back-to-back showers. Tankless water heaters cost more to install upfront, but they last longer and use less energy, because they only heat water once someone turns on the faucet.

Ask if the home's main sewer line has been cleared out in recent memory or, if the home is on a septic system, when the septic tank was installed and when it was last cleaned out. A septic system can last twenty to forty years or more, but they're expensive to replace.

Electrical

Electrical faults and malfunctions caused 13 percent of all residential fires between 2012 and 2016, according to the National Fire Protection Association, so it's essential that your home's wiring is in good, safe working order.

Like the plumbing, a home's electrical system is largely hidden from view, but you can still check visible wiring, outlets, and the circuit breaker for obvious issues, and hire an electrical inspector if you see any potential problems. Here are some things you might want to ask about or look for:

- What is the capacity of the home's main electric panel? Newer homes are usually set up for 100- to 200-amp service. An older home may still have 60-amp service, which you'll probably want to upgrade.
- Is the circuit breaker clearly labeled with individual breakers for important appliances like the furnace, refrigerator, or water heater? Older homes could still have a fuse box—another borderline antiquity you'll probably want to upgrade.
- Are there GFCI outlets in water-prone areas like the bathroom and kitchen?
- Are there enough properly grounded three-prong outlets per room? Some older homes only have one or two outlets in rooms that haven't been updated.
- Are there any signs of active knob-and-tube wiring? In the early twentieth century, this popular wiring technique used ceramic knobs to run cloth-insulated wires through the wall cavities, and you may still encounter it in an old home. Ceramic knob remnants are nothing to worry about, and even active knob-and-tube wiring is not *necessarily* unsafe, but it is definitely not up to modern standards, and some insurance companies won't insure a home with this type of wiring. Replacing it will cost a few thousand dollars.
- If the home was built (or updated) between 1965 and 1972, are there signs of silvery aluminum wiring? Copper was scarce during the Vietnam War, so many homes of the era were built using aluminum wire instead. The softer metal can create fire hazards at junction boxes and other connections.

Structural

A home's timber, stone, or brick framing should last a lifetime, but it's worth inspecting wood for signs of rot and masonry or foundations for cracks and gaps. The roof, meanwhile, is a critical home system in itself, keeping everything inside sheltered from the elements. If you see roof shingles starting to cup or curl like frying bacon, you're going to have to replace it soon.

Appliances

Most homes are sold with the appliances in place, though sometimes you may need to supply your own refrigerator or washer and dryer. Appliances are big-ticket items that will obviously play a big role in your day-to-day home life, so it's worth checking their age and condition.

THINGS YOU CAN CHANGE, AND THINGS YOU CAN'T

Learn to Recognize Possibility—and Its Limits

As you tour homes for sale, try to look beyond the surface. Don't get distracted by the decor—none of it will be there when you move in. If you can approach the homes you tour with a bit of vision, you'll have an edge over the many buyers who simply can't mentally place themselves and their lives inside a drab or quirky home.

Whether it's worth paying that price, as opposed to paying more now for a picture-perfect home, is for you to decide. But don't immediately write off a home that doesn't fit your ideal.

THINGS YOU CAN CHANGE

- **Cosmetics:** Realtors beg their buyers not to get hung up on outdated fixtures, tacky carpeting, or purple walls. As long as it still functions properly, virtually any cosmetic feature can be changed (or lived with until you have the money to upgrade). A simple coat of paint, in particular, is a cheap, transformational DIY project. So try to use your imagination and look beyond the seller's style.
- **Site grade:** The way a home sits on its lot is an underappreciated trait. Ideally, you want the yard to slope gently away from the structure on all sides, so water drains away from the house, not into it. If that's not the case, it's usually easy enough for a landscaper to regrade the lot so you don't risk ending up with a wet, moldy basement. If the home is on a hill, and no amount of

regrading will help, remedies like a French drain can still protect your basement from water infiltration.

- **Energy and efficiency:** Don't be afraid of a drafty old home. Adding insulation to the attic, basement, and walls can drastically improve energy efficiency, and many states offer rebates or no-interest loans to help pay for it. Many homes can accommodate rooftop solar panels to produce renewable energy; if yours can't, it's getting easier to sign up for a community solar plan or to select 100 percent renewable energy from your utility. If a home is heated with oil, it's possible to install an electric heat pump to reduce oil use.
- **Landscaping:** Nature takes time, but you can create the yard of your dreams through thoughtful planting and pruning if there's enough room to do so. Don't let an overgrown or unkempt yard deter you.

Getting Some Rays

If a home has solar panels, ask how old they are, and whether they're owned or leased. If they are owned outright, they'll provide you with free, renewable electricity for the life of the panels—typically about twenty years. Leased panels are owned and maintained by a solar company, which sells you the power they produce at a slight discount to the going rate from the electric company.

THINGS YOU CAN *USUALLY* CHANGE

- **Layout:** It's typically possible to knock down walls during a renovation to improve a floor plan's flow, but not always. If you have your heart set on opening up the kitchen to the living area, ask a contractor or structural engineer to verify whether that will be possible, or what your options are if it's a load-bearing wall.

- **Square footage:** It's rarely easy or cheap to do—you can't just buy square footage at the hardware store, after all—but there's often a way to squeeze some more living space out of a home if needed. That may mean finishing a basement, dormering an attic, or building an addition. Even adding a deck or patio can increase your usable space for a good portion of the year. Such solutions may not be an option in a condo, unless there's potential for a loft space, for example. Even a single-family home may be maxed out if every nook and cranny has been updated and town zoning won't allow you to expand the building's footprint any closer to neighboring properties.

- **Foundation issues:** It's not always a sign of a major problem, but a cracked or damaged foundation can definitely be a big concern for a buyer. But as any contractor will tell you, "Anything can be fixed with enough money." That's not to say that you want to be the one to fix a damaged foundation! It could cost tens of thousands of dollars—or more—to address, or could be a symptom of other costly problems. But even this most dreaded of home issues can generally be remedied if necessary.

THINGS YOU CAN'T CHANGE

- **Location:** As discussed in Chapter 6, location is everything in real estate. Where that home sits is where it will stay, and that will define your public school system, your tax rate, and even the air you breathe. Getting beyond the neighborhood into site specifics, a corner lot offers lots of light and views—but it also means having less privacy and two sidewalks to shovel. A hilltop location is always nice, but it may mean hiking uphill to get home or braving a slippery road in winter. And if it takes forty-five minutes to get downtown from your location, that's probably not going to change.

- **Acreage:** You can add square footage by building an addition, but only if there's room on your lot to do so. Unless your neighbor's home goes up for sale (and you somehow can afford to buy it), the size of your lot is what you've got.

- **Orientation:** If you like waking up to morning light, then look for a home with east-facing bedrooms. Love an afternoon glow in the living room or kitchen? Look for windows that face the south or southwest. If the garage takes up the entire south side of the home, meanwhile, you're going to miss out on a lot of sunlight.

- **Elevation:** While you can address your site grade to try to prevent a wet basement, there's no changing the elevation of your lot. Low-lying areas may be prone to flooding (and may require flood insurance as a mortgage condition), and as sea levels rise, that risk will only intensify. It is possible, though costly, to elevate your home out of danger by raising the entire structure and all mechanical systems above the floodplain. But that won't stop the road leading to your home from getting submerged during a storm surge, along with much of the surrounding neighborhood.

- **Ceiling height:** Homes built during frugal times, such as the 1700s or the 1940s, often have low ceilings that can feel a bit claustrophobic. Unless there's a drop ceiling you can remove, you're generally stuck with the ceiling height you see. (Sometimes, though, it's possible to strip the drywall or plaster and expose the ceiling joists—as well as any wiring and plumbing—adding a few more inches and a rustic industrial look overhead.)

Chapter 8

Making an Offer

You may spend three short weeks or three long months looking at homes for sale before you find one that makes your heart race and your brain nod in sage agreement. But no matter how long or slow the journey, things are about to start moving much more quickly. Everything you've done so far has been in anticipation of this moment, getting you prepared to pounce when you find the right home.

But just because you're equipped to meet the occasion doesn't mean it will be easy. Placing an offer is a big financial step as well as an emotional leap—one that leaves you vulnerable to rejection. In this chapter, we'll discuss the mechanics and the art of making an offer, including the timeline, negotiating strategies, and various protections you can write into the contract.

YOU LOVE THE HOUSE— NOW WHAT?

What to Do When You Find "Your Home"

You've found the one. Your heart leaps at the thought, your imagination aflame with visions of your life within these walls: A winter morning curled up by the fireplace; a barbecue on the deck next summer; a joyful, boisterous Thanksgiving five years from now. All of these scenes play out in your mind, flashes of a future nearly within your reach. This is the place for you.

When you find Your Home, it can be an intoxicating rush. The pitter-patter of your racing heart is incredibly important to the process—but a little bit dangerous too.

That feeling is a crucial courage builder to help you go through with the next momentous step: committing what is likely your life's savings to purchase this box of rooms—one that will likely demand much of your time, money, and energy for years to come. It's hard to take that kind of leap without an emotional incentive.

And yet those emotions can seriously cloud your judgment and decision making. When you're about to purchase something that costs hundreds of thousands of dollars, you want the logical bookkeeper in your brain calling the shots.

Here are some tips on listening to both your heart and mind as you prepare to make an offer.

Take Another Look

Unless your local market is so competitive at the moment that you feel compelled to place an offer the same day (in overheated seller's markets, some homes literally go under agreement before the end of the first open house), you should always go back for one more thorough look at a home before placing an offer.

Try to shed the dreamy wonder of your first impression and approach this tour with a little more scrutiny, taking a hard look at some of the less glamorous details we discussed in Chapter 7: the furnace, the pipes, the foundation. Flip all the light switches. Turn on the heat and the air conditioner to ensure they work. Flush the toilets, test all the faucets, and taste the tap water. Try to imagine the home under different conditions—those steep stone steps might be fine in May, but what about when they're covered in ice come January?

Get Familiar with the Home's Flaws

That doesn't mean you shouldn't buy the home if you find potential issues upon closer examination—almost every home will have some. You just need to be aware of those issues, so you're not taken by surprise. Embrace the home's imperfections, and start including them in your daydreams of homeownership (e.g., "Before we move in, we'll replace the vanity in the upstairs bath and paint the bedrooms.").

If the home needs big or urgent repairs, sit with that idea, and keep those costs in mind; you may want to lower the price you're willing to pay by the cost of any necessary upgrades.

Could You Learn to Love It?

Sometimes it's not your brain that needs convincing but your heart. Maybe you've been searching for a long time, and you've finally found a place that meets all of your must-haves, delivers on most of your wants, and fits your price range, but just...doesn't excite you.

That's okay. Your first home doesn't have to be your forever home. But it would be nice if your heart could get on board with the idea. So try to pinpoint exactly what is leaving you unenthused and whether it's something you could change (would repainting the drab, beige exterior make you happier to call this place home?) or something that will quietly gnaw at you for years to come (if you've always dreamed of owning a gable-peaked farmhouse, a boxy ranch just may not make you happy, no matter how practical it may be).

No Regrets

The majority of new homeowners had no regrets about their recent home purchase, according to an April 2021 *Bankrate* survey—but 64 percent of millennial home buyers had at least one regret. If you're looking to avoid their fate, the most common lament (16 percent) was underestimating the cost of maintenance and other homeowner expenses. Buying a home that was too small (9 percent), in a bad location (8 percent), or too big (7 percent) were some of the other commonly expressed regrets.

GET READY TO MAKE AN OFFER

Once your head and your heart are on the same page, act quickly. Clear your schedule; it's time to ask your Realtor to submit an offer on your behalf.

Got your lender's preapproval letter handy? This is when you'll need it. Also make sure you have enough cash in your checking account to make a good-faith deposit (we'll explain how much you'll need later in the chapter).

Lastly, brace yourself: You're about to put yourself out there, and even though you've now fallen in love with this home, there's a chance you won't get it. Almost half of home buyers (45 percent) make offers on multiple homes before ultimately purchasing one, according to *Zillow*, and losing out on a home you love can be both frustrating and emotionally devastating. It's easier said than done, but try to keep your expectations in check.

While your agent will prepare your offer for you, typically just customizing a standard template, there are plenty of variables to consider including in it—things that can protect your interests and make your offer stand out to the seller. It all starts with the price, which we'll discuss next.

HOW MUCH SHOULD YOU OFFER?

Not Too High, Not Too Low

There are a lot of ways to make an offer more enticing to a seller, but none speaks as loudly as pure and simple price. Still, you don't want to overpay or commit yourself to a future of financial stress. Ideally, you want to offer just enough to win the house, and not a dollar more. But how do you figure out what that price is?

Trust Your Realtor

Your real estate agent should have a good sense of what it will take to get your offer accepted. That figure will depend on market conditions, the home itself, and whether there are multiple offers coming in at the same time.

To do this, your agent will start with comparable sales (called "comps") to see what similar nearby homes have sold for recently, and determine an approximate baseline for the home's market value. Then they'll make some adjustments based on factors like market momentum—they'll know if their colleagues' listings have been attracting a lot of over-asking-price offers, for example, or if another client was able to secure an accepted offer with relative ease—or the home's price bracket. (In many markets, competition is fiercest in the lower, more affordable price ranges, while luxury-priced homes tend to linger.)

Your Realtor can tell you what the home ought to sell for and what it will probably take to get your offer accepted; those figures may not be the same, depending on the market. Then it's up to you to decide whether you're comfortable with that price, whether you'd like to try offering a little less (even if it means a greater risk of losing out on the home), or if you want to submit an even higher, can't-miss offer because you absolutely must have this home.

In a slow or normal market, your first offer doesn't have to be your last. You can submit an offer below the asking price, and as long as it's not insultingly low, the seller may come back with a counteroffer. Say the list price is $400,000, and you offer $380,000; if there hasn't been too much interest from other buyers or any higher offers, the seller might counter your offer with a price of $390,000. At that point, you might want to just grab that lower price (before any other buyers show interest), or try a counterbid of your own—say, $385,000.

In a more competitive market, your Realtor can ask the listing agent if there are any other offers being considered—in which case, you should put forward your best and highest offer upfront, because you probably won't get a second chance. When there are five offers on the table, and three of them are well over the asking price, a seller isn't going to bother making counteroffers. A multiple-offer scenario can be incredibly stressful and nerve-shredding, but we'll discuss some strategies for navigating a hot market later in this chapter.

Over and Under

Whether you can compete with a bid under asking price or need to beat the list price just to be considered will depend on how an individual home is priced, as well as broader market factors like supply and demand. And those factors can flip quickly.

In the first few months of 2021, for example, home buyer demand was so great, and the supply of homes for sale so limited, that over 1,500 homes in Austin, Texas, sold for at least $100,000 over the asking price, according to Redfin. The year before, that happened just twenty-two times.

Find the Goldilocks Price

While the market will dictate the ultimate sales price of a home, you have to put forward a number that you're comfortable with. Even in a hot market, don't base your offer on what you think other people will bid; base it on what you're willing to pay, independent of what anyone else is doing.

Why? Because if there's a couple out there who's already had five or six offers rejected after a year of house hunting, they may be at their breaking point—willing to wildly overpay just to be done with the process. That's beyond your control, and it's not a battle you want to fight.

So how do you settle on that perfect price—the one that's competitive enough to win, but not so high that you'll condemn yourself to years of PB&J dinners? Here's how you know your offer is just right: if you'd be happy to get the home at that price and relieved if you don't. It's a fine line, but it can be found, and you'll start to feel increasing unease as you tiptoe beyond it.

What does that look like in real, numerical terms? Here's one example: Let's say you really want that $400,000 home. Your agent tells you there are several other offers coming in, so you'll need to make the most competitive bid you can. You're thinking of offering $420,000. But if you did, and someone else got the house for $422,000…would you be upset that you didn't offer a little bit more?

If that's the case, increase your bid to $422,000, assuming you're qualified to. Find the price point at which, if you lost out by just $1,000, you wouldn't beat yourself up for not offering more. (We'll discuss more strategies for navigating seller's and buyer's markets later in this chapter.)

DEPOSITS AND TIMING

The Ball Is Officially Rolling

A lot happens in quick succession once you decide to make an offer on a home. You'll be forced to make some big decisions fairly quickly, and you'll inevitably find yourself waiting anxiously for a call or text from your agent. It's also time to dip into the cash you've been carefully saving, which feels like its own very big step.

The specifics will vary by state, and the timing can be even more hectic in a seller's market, but here are some of the things you'll need to do or think about in the next few days.

Decide How Much "Earnest Money" to Include

When you place an offer to buy a home, you'll generally include a good-faith deposit, called earnest money, to illustrate that you're a serious buyer.

It's not unlike providing your credit card number to hold a restaurant or hotel reservation. You're asking the seller to take their home off the market and reserve it just for you; if you were to back out and cancel without warning, it would create a major inconvenience and a potential financial blow for them. So putting a small deposit down shows that you intend to follow through.

Granted, that "small" deposit is usually a few thousand dollars—typically about 1–2 percent of the home price, and sometimes more, depending on what's customary in your local market. So on a $300,000 home, you can expect to attach to your offer a good-faith deposit in the neighborhood of $3,000 to $6,000.

Unlike closing costs and other fees, however, earnest money isn't an extra expense. If the deal goes through, your deposit will be applied toward your down payment or closing costs.

Earnest money is generally delivered along with the offer or sales contract in the form of a personal check, and the money isn't given directly to the seller. Even if they accept your offer, the check is held by a third party, such as your agent or a title company, and it's deposited into a neutral escrow account (if it's deposited at all).

Making an Offer

Your agent will help you put together a formal purchase offer, which will include key details such as the address of the property, the price you're willing to pay for it, the date you wish to close, how much earnest money is included, and how much time the seller has to review your offer before it expires—typically one to three days. For example, you may make your offer valid for forty-eight hours, or until 5 p.m. on Tuesday. (Some states have default deadlines; in California, for example, a seller has three days to accept an offer unless otherwise noted.)

Your offer may also include some contingencies, which are conditions that need to be met for the deal to go through. For example, your offer may be contingent on your ability to secure a mortgage. (We'll get deeper into contingencies in the next section.) Other more granular details include how expenses like closing costs, utility bills, and property taxes will be divided between you and the seller.

Acceptance, Refusal, or Something In Between

The seller and the listing agent will review your offer along with any others they receive. They can then either accept it as written, reject it outright, or make a counteroffer.

If you're not even in the ballpark—perhaps your offer was much too low, or they received several better offers—you'll learn that your offer was rejected, and it's back to the drawing board. If the seller accepts and signs your offer exactly as is, congratulations! You've got yourself a legal purchase and sale agreement—a binding contract to purchase the home.

More commonly, though, the seller may express interest in moving forward with you but under slightly different terms. Their agent may present yours with a counteroffer that seeks to raise the price, adjust the timeline, or remove some contingencies (or add some of their own). Now you're the one with a deadline. You'll have a specified amount of time to accept, refuse, or counteroffer. We'll discuss counteroffers and the negotiation process later in this chapter.

Even a Perfect Offer Can Fall Short

A seller is under no obligation to accept your offer, even if it's the only one they receive and even if it's at or above the asking price. If they suddenly get cold feet about selling their home or decide they want to hold out for a better price, they're entitled to do so.

Once your offer is accepted and signed, it's a binding legal contract, and if you back out without good reason, you'll have to forfeit your earnest money. However, if you included some contingencies in your offer, you can still get out of the deal (with your earnest money) if those conditions aren't met. In the next section, we'll look at some of those important escape clauses.

WHAT ARE CONTINGENCIES?

Locate Your Nearest Emergency Exit

When you submit an offer to buy a home, it's a legal document—and if the seller accepts it, you're entering into a binding contract. Your real estate agent or attorney can craft the offer to include a number of emergency escape hatches, called contingencies, to protect you.

A contingency clause specifies a condition that must be met before the sale can go forward, making the sale "contingent" on that outcome. If that condition isn't met, you're legally allowed to walk away from the sale with your earnest money or renegotiate the contract.

COMMON CONTINGENCIES

Theoretically, you could include just about anything as a contingency, but here are the most common ones.

Financing

Almost every first-time buyer needs to include a mortgage contingency. This states that the sale depends on your ability to successfully secure a home loan—so if your financing falls through, the deal is off. Without this clause in place, if you were denied a mortgage at the last minute, you would either have to find a new funding source fast, or pull out of the sale and forfeit your earnest money.

If you include a mortgage contingency in your offer (and you probably ought to), it's crucial to attach your lender's preapproval letter. That way the seller can see that, barring some drastic turn of events, your financing is already arranged and all but guaranteed to go through.

Home Inspection

Another must-have contingency for most first-time buyers is the chance to conduct a home inspection and to reconsider or renegotiate the sale based on the results.

For example, your inspection contingency may state that you have ten days to complete a home inspection. If the home inspector finds an issue—say, that the roof needs replacing—you could ask the seller to fix the problem before closing or to drop the price by some amount (such as the estimated cost of the repair).

The seller may not agree to repair the issue or adjust the price, but if you can't come to terms, you still have the right to walk away. And if the inspection turns up something truly daunting, this contingency allows you to legally back out of the sale.

Appraisal Inspection

If you're using a mortgage, you may want to include an appraisal contingency, and here's why: Your lender will require an independent appraiser to assess the home's market value before they finalize your loan. (They want to make sure the property is worth what you're paying for it, since you're using their money to buy it.) If the appraisal comes in below the agreed-upon price, it can throw your mortgage application out of whack—you would need to apply for a larger loan or make up the difference in cash (neither of which may be possible if you're already stretching your budget). This contingency allows you to back out of the sale or renegotiate the price if the appraisal comes in below the contract price.

Home Sale

As a first-time buyer, you won't need to include a home sale contingency in your offer. Buyers who are trading up from one home to another typically need the proceeds from their current home to afford their next home. This clause allows them to back out or postpone the sale if they're unable to finalize the sale of their current home.

Suitable Housing

A seller will sometimes include a contingency of their own, stating that the home sale is dependent on the seller finding suitable housing. That means the seller can pull out of the sale—or, more likely, delay it—if they're unable to find and purchase a new home of their own before closing. Ask your agent about ways to structure this contingency that will protect you while still offering the seller some reassurance.

Other Contingencies

You can include other contingencies as needed, and the seller may include some of their own. Your lender may insist on a contingency that says the sale depends on your ability to secure homeowner's insurance for the property before closing. To minimize confusion and frustration, any contingency should be specific in its terms and its timeline. (The seller will not want to wait eight months for you to find home insurance.)

Sellers don't love buyer contingencies, since they inject some uncertainty into the contract, giving buyers a chance to wriggle out of the deal or negotiate a lower price. But in a normal market, basic contingencies such as the home inspection and financing contingency are very much par for the course.

That changes in a seller's market, however, where sellers have more leverage because they can choose among multiple offers. In those situations, every contingency added will make the seller a bit more wary of your offer and more likely to take another offer without any wild cards in it. We'll discuss some ways to make your offer more attractive without putting yourself at risk at the end of this chapter.

NEGOTIATION AND COUNTEROFFERS

The Price Is Just the Beginning

Just about every aspect of a home sale can be negotiated. That starts with the price, of course, but also up for discussion is whether the sale includes the refrigerator or those custom light fixtures you swooned over at the open house.

Your initial offer can be considered the starting point of negotiations. If the seller comes back with a counteroffer, then you can accept it or continue negotiating further. Aside from the boundaries of human patience, there's no limit to how many times you can go back and forth.

There's much to be gained from negotiating a better deal, but be aware: Every moment that passes without a signed contract is one in which another buyer can swoop in. If the seller gets a better offer while you're contemplating their counteroffer, they can abruptly withdraw that offer and sign a purchase contract with the other buyer, leaving you back on the sidelines.

Since time is of the essence, your agent may negotiate with the listing agent verbally in order to hammer out a few points of contention before submitting a follow-up counteroffer. Still, verbal acceptance is no substitute for a signature on the dotted line.

WHAT'S NEGOTIABLE?

From the opening bid of your offer to the seller's third counteroffer, here are some of the things that are commonly negotiated in real estate transactions.

Price

Naturally, the price is the biggest negotiating point in any purchase agreement. Money doesn't just talk; it tends to shout over anything else you may haggle over.

Some counteroffers may include nuanced negotiations about the finer points of the contract, but often they will come down to price: You offer $390,000 on a $400,000 home, and the seller counters with $397,500. You can accept that discount off the asking price or try again, perhaps countering back with $395,000.

And even after you've settled on a sale price, you may still have a chance to negotiate it lower, depending on how the home inspection or appraisal goes (provided your offer contains those contingencies). If the buyer accepts your counteroffer of $395,000, for instance, but the bank's appraiser later assesses the home's market value at $390,000, you may be able to bargain the price down.

Timing

Another thing that may be up for negotiation is the timetable. You may be looking for a faster closing if, for example, you need to be out of your apartment before your lease ends, or you're hoping to save money with a shorter rate-lock period. The seller, meanwhile, may want to push the closing date farther back, perhaps giving their children enough time to finish out the school year before moving.

If you're flexible on your timing—whether you're renting on a month-to-month lease or living with family or friends—use that to your advantage. Ask your agent to find out what kind of timeline would work best for the seller, and be as accommodating as you can, so the seller may be more willing to cut you a better deal or concede to some of your other requests.

Repairs

If your home inspection turns up any issues, you can ask the seller to fix the problems before closing or to lower the price to make up for the cost of repairs. Unless it's a real buyer's market, you probably won't want to nitpick about every little thing. But it's not unreasonable to ask a seller to get a leaking pipe fixed before you move in, for example, or to repair safety issues like a rotting stair tread on the deck. (We'll discuss the home inspection in detail in Chapter 9.)

Contingencies

A seller may counter your offer with one that removes some key contingencies. If they have a competing cash offer, for example, they may only want to entertain your offer if you're willing to remove the appraisal or financing contingency. Even if you're 99 percent sure that your mortgage will go through, think long and hard before you agree to a contract without those protections.

However, it's not just the inclusion or exclusion of certain contingencies that can be negotiated, but also how they're defined.

For example, instead of a traditional home inspection contingency, you may offer or accept a "void only" inspection contingency. This permits you to conduct a full home inspection, but it limits your recourse if you don't like what the inspection turns up. You're only allowed to void the sale entirely based on the inspection results, not to negotiate repairs or a lower price.

Appliances and Exclusions

In some real estate listings, you'll notice a section called exclusions. These are items the seller intends to take with them when they move, even though they may seem like part of the home, such as the curtains or a chandelier.

As you go back and forth on price, the exclusion of big-ticket items can help offset a price drop in the seller's eyes. For example, perhaps they'll agree to your below-asking offer—but only if they're able to take their new refrigerator and washer-dryer combo with them.

You *Can* Take It with You

Sellers are liable to exclude all kinds of things from a home sale, from high-end appliances or custom light fixtures to more sentimental items, like a stained glass window hanging or favorite flowers and shrubs in the yard. If there's something you love about a home and it isn't fastened to the wall or floor, make sure you're clear about whether it's staying or going.

Closing Costs

As mentioned in Chapter 4, first-time buyers without much cash on hand can sometimes negotiate a seller's credit or concession toward closing costs. In a buyer's market, a seller may make an out-of-pocket contribution toward the closing costs just to ensure that the transaction goes through. But a seller's concession can often be structured in a way where the buyer simply pays a correspondingly higher price for the home.

For example, if the agreed-upon sale price is $400,000, you could ask the seller to pay $4,000 toward your closing costs in exchange for a higher sale price of $404,000. As long as you're qualified to borrow that much, and the home appraises that high, it effectively allows you to finance your closing costs into the thirty-year mortgage.

Earnest Money

If your initial deposit is on the small side, a seller may request that you put down more earnest money as something of an insurance policy to make sure the deal goes through—particularly if there are a lot of contingencies in your offer that could derail the purchase agreement.

TWO SIDES, ONE STORY

Remember that, even though you and the seller are approaching the transaction from different sides of the table, you do share a common goal: getting to closing. You want to buy their home, and they want to sell it. The rest is just details.

Having almost everything in a home sale up for negotiation allows for some creative ways to make your offer more appealing to sellers in a tight market, or to exercise your own leverage in a buyer's market. In the next section, we'll look at some techniques for each.

TIPS FOR NAVIGATING BUYER'S AND SELLER'S MARKETS

How to Make Your Offer More Enticing—or More Advantageous

Real estate is more stable than a lot of investments, but it's still subject to the basic economic principle of supply and demand.

If there are lots of homes for sale, and few people can or want to buy one, prices tend to fall, and buyers have the upper hand in negotiations. That's a buyer's market. When there aren't enough homes for sale to meet home buyer demand, that creates a seller's market—where multiple buyers may be forced to compete for each home, all trying to outbid one another.

Because real estate is so dependent on location, you could be contending with a seller's market even while friends in another state seem to have the upper hand as buyers. Other times, though, housing markets across the entire country seem to move in lockstep with one another.

One of the most widespread buyer's markets in recent memory was in the wake of the financial crisis of 2008–2011. A surge in foreclosures flooded the housing market with homes for sale at a time when many people couldn't afford to buy one. That put buyers in the driver's seat.

To see a nationwide seller's market in action, meanwhile, look no further than 2020 and early 2021, when a combination of ravenous home buyer demand and a shortage of homes for sale stoked fierce competition among buyers and bidding wars that drove prices up to record levels.

Home Buyers Can Expect Continued Competition

Experts expect strong home buyer demand to continue for several years more as millennials, currently the largest generation in the United States, age into their early and mid-thirties—typically the peak home buying years. However, if there's enough new home construction to relieve the housing shortage, the overall market could return to a healthy balance.

TIPS FOR COMPETING IN A SELLER'S MARKET

In a seller's market, homeowners have all the leverage. Making your offer stand out is all about cash and contingencies: All things being equal, most sellers would prefer an all-cash offer with no contingencies in it, because that's the deal that's guaranteed to go through without delays or complications. Here are some tips to make your offer more competitive.

Go Big with Your Down Payment

In a hot market, cash-starved first-time home buyers are forced to compete with existing homeowners, who can sell their current home into the market frenzy for big bucks. That means sellers will be receiving offers with large down payments (and maybe even all-cash offers). The larger the down payment, the less likely a sale is to get upended by a low appraisal or financing hiccup. So anything you can add to your down payment will help you compete.

Get Pre-Underwritten

Getting fully preapproved for a mortgage is the bare minimum in a seller's market. But, as discussed in Chapter 4, some lenders even offer pre-underwriting. Getting pre-underwritten means the lender has already sent your application through the full underwriting process, and you've been approved for a loan.

That's not to say your financing couldn't still unravel, but it's much less likely to at that point. So some real estate agents encourage clients to get pre-underwritten and then drop the financing contingency from their offer, to make their bid more competitive with cash buyers.

Conduct a Pre-Inspection or a Void-Only Inspection

Another clause sellers would prefer not to see on an offer is the inspection contingency—after all, this gives you the chance to negotiate a lower price if the inspection turns up problems. If there are two offers at the same price, and one has no inspection contingency, the seller is going to choose that one.

And yet, forgoing an inspection is an extremely risky move that most agents do not recommend. Skipping the inspection can have devastating consequences. You don't want to spend your life's savings on a home only to find out later that it's riddled with termite damage or the foundation is failing, and it will take another $100,000 to fix it.

There are two ways around this. A "void-only" inspection contingency informs the seller that you won't try to negotiate a lower price based on the inspection findings, but it does allow you to pull out of the sale if anything truly terrible emerges during the inspection.

If you want to drop the home inspection contingency entirely, you can sometimes arrange a pre-inspection. This means you pay a home inspector to tour the home with you even before you make an offer; that way, you'll at least know what you're getting into.

This approach can get expensive, however, since you may have to pay an inspector multiple times before you land a winning bid. And not all sellers are amenable to the idea, since there may be multiple buyers trying to arrange a three-hour inspection; even then, though, it should be possible to bring an inspector or contractor friend along with you on a private showing, when they can at least check for major problems.

Add an Escalation Clause

Have you ever placed a bid on *eBay*? You make an initial offer that's just above the current high bid, but you also enter the most you're willing to pay for the item. Then, if someone outbids you later on, your bid amount automatically increases to put you back on top until you hit your limit.

An escalation clause in a home offer is similar—it will automatically increase your offer price to beat the next-highest bidder up to a certain point (or even indefinitely, which is a winning but dangerous strategy). This strategy lays all of your cards on the table, telling the seller exactly how high you're willing to go, so it should really only be used if you're certain that a home will receive a flurry of competing offers. And if several buyers submit offers with escalation clauses, the bidding war can race out of control pretty quickly, so consult your real estate agent and instruct them to be careful when wielding this tool.

Use What You Have

Even if you don't have a big down payment or an infinite budget, consider your assets.

For example, if you're flexible on timing, make that clear to the listing agent and seller; you may be the only competitive buyer who can also offer a later closing date.

If the seller is nervous about not having enough time to move into their next home, offer a "lease-back" arrangement—where the seller rents the home from you for a week or a month after closing, giving them some more time to move out.

If you or your family owns a landscaping or snow plow company, you could try offering the seller a year of free services at their new home. Anything you can do to sweeten the deal for the seller (within the boundaries of fair housing laws) is worth a try.

Shop Homes Below Your Price Range

When homes are routinely selling for over the asking price—when even offering $200,000 over the list price is no guarantee that you'll win a bidding war—look at homes lower down in your price range. That way, you can comfortably come in with a strong offer well above asking.

TIPS FOR A BUYER'S MARKET

If you're house hunting in a buyer's market, you're in luck. You'll have more time to think through big decisions, and less competition for the home you love. Since life events don't wait for an advantageous real estate market, some homeowners will be desperate to sell and ready to bargain. You can flex your strength by asking for a lower price or negotiating other concessions.

Bid Low (but Not Too Low)

In a buyer's market, you can usually underbid the asking price, especially if a home has been sitting on the market for a few weeks without much interest. That means you can even shop for homes slightly out of your price range, and make an offer 5 percent to 10 percent below the asking price.

Ask your agent for advice on how low you can safely go with your offer. Because even in a buyer's market, a truly "lowball" bid may insult a seller. (It is their home, after all—perhaps the place where they raised their children or grew up themselves—and it's valuable to them.)

Ask for Concessions

With fewer buyers about, sellers may be willing to sweeten the deal to get you to buy their home. That starts with a seller's credit or concession to help pay for some or all of the closing costs. (In a buyer's market, you probably won't have to offset this with a higher sale price.)

But you can also ask for other concessions. For example, the seller may agree to pay your first six months of condo fees or property taxes, or to let you keep any remaining heating oil in the oil tank for free. If the sellers have a piece of artwork or furniture in the home that you love the look of, ask about including it in the sale.

Use Your Contingencies

This is no time to cut contingencies from your offer. Have your Realtor include the full complement of contingency clauses to protect your interests and keep your options open.

Negotiate Repairs

If the home inspection turns up any issues, from an outdated electrical box to cracked plaster, you can ask the seller to fix those problems before the closing date or to lower the price by the amount it will take to repair them. If you're the only interested buyer they've had so far, they're probably not going to argue the point this far along in the process.

Don't Dawdle on a Dream

Buyer's market or not, desirable homes will sell quickly if they're priced right. If you find the perfect home for you at a price you like, there's no reason to get greedy or drag your feet—jump on it.

Chapter 9

Your Offer Is Accepted: The Countdown to Closing

Have you ever been waiting for a taxi or a train, and seen one approaching in the distance...only to crumple in disappointment as it zips past you without stopping? There's a chance that a home or two will slip through your fingers. It's disappointing, to say the least.

But even if it takes a few tries, you'll eventually get an offer accepted. And at that point, you're essentially aboard the express train to homeownership. There's still a lot to do—but it's all going to happen in quick, fairly orderly succession. And unless you see a need to get off at a different stop (or even jump off the train), you should arrive at your destination right on schedule.

As you hurtle toward homeownership, here's what to expect between now and closing.

THE HOME INSPECTION

"What Would You Say Is Your Biggest Weakness?"

One of the most important steps between getting an offer accepted and closing is the home inspection—and you'll want to get it scheduled right away. Your offer may stipulate that you have a limited time frame to get an inspection—for example, one week or ten days—so it's helpful to start researching home inspectors well before you need to hire one.

You can expect to pay between $300 and $600 for a home inspection, depending on the size and age of the home, your region, and whether the inspector offers additional services, certifications, or expertise. You're probably none too eager to shell out more money right now, but that fee represents one of the best values in real estate: a few hundred dollars now can save you thousands or even tens of thousands of dollars by alerting you to any big, unexpected problems.

Choosing a Home Inspector

Online reviews are a good starting point when searching for a reputable home inspector, but they have their limitations. If you have friends who recently bought a home in the area, ask whether they were happy with the inspector they chose.

Ask potential home inspectors if you can accompany them on the inspection. Most will be happy to have you trail them. Check whether they have professional accreditations, and look for inspectors with years of experience with both the area and the type of home you're buying.

Set Your Expectations

Your inspector should spend two to four hours in and around the home, with much of that time spent in the basement or utility room, where the home's major systems are headquartered.

The inspector will evaluate every square foot of the property, inside and out, and alert you to any potential problems—from signs of rot beneath a windowsill to an improperly installed sink drain. After the inspection, they should provide you with a comprehensive report that details their findings, including photos that illustrate any potential concerns.

There are things a home inspector can't do, however. They can only comment on what's immediately accessible and visible to them (they can't see through walls), so they won't be able to say definitively if there's a problem lurking behind the drywall or under the floorboards—only whether there are warning signs that might warrant further investigation by a contractor. They cannot tell you whether or not to buy the home (though you can always try asking if they'd let their own kid go through with such a purchase). And though you'll be tempted to ask how much it will cost to fix a problem they see, home inspectors generally aren't allowed to offer price guidance or recommend tradespeople, either.

Inside and Out

Even if you're buying a condo, the inspector should spend plenty of time outside of your unit, walking the grounds and common areas and assessing the condition of the entire property. After all, you'll be a co-owner of the whole building and responsible for a share of any big expenses. If it looks like the complex will need a new roof soon, you'll want to be prepared for that.

Attend the Home Inspection

Tagging along with the home inspector is a great way to learn all about the home you're buying—not just the problems with it but also how it works and why it was built the way it was. They'll point out and explain any suspected issue, how big a deal it is, and what else to watch out for. If you don't understand something, ask for an explanation—home inspectors are quite accustomed to communicating with anxious first-time home buyers.

Read and Keep the Report

A home inspection is educational in nature—an act of information gathering. The final report will offer a wealth of information and recommendations, but how you use it is up to you.

For example, if the inspection turns up issues that weren't previously disclosed by the seller, such as outdated wiring or faulty plumbing, you can use the report as a negotiating tool and ask the seller to either fix the problem or lower the price by a commensurate amount.

Even if you don't use the report as a basis for negotiations, it's invaluable to you as a new homeowner. The report will typically include a list of suggested repairs or action items, which you can use to prioritize home improvements and plan for future renovations.

Even in new construction, a home inspection can turn up issues—anything from missing switch plates to disconnected pipes. You can use the inspection report to create a punch list of items for your builder to address before closing.

Hire Specialists As Needed

A home inspector is a generalist—like a family doctor or general practitioner—and while they can recognize signs of trouble, they're not equipped to fully diagnose some specific issues.

If your inspector finds signs of termite damage, for example, or a troublesome crack in the foundation, you'll want to get a pest inspector or a structural engineer (respectively) to check out the specific problem. If there's evidence of mold or mildew, meanwhile, you'll want to hire a mold specialist to determine how bad it is and how much it will cost to remedy it. If there appears to be an issue with the home's wiring, you'll want a licensed electrician to check it out.

Depending on what they find, your home inspector may recommend other inspections, such as a septic tank or sewer line inspection. In homes with a basement, you'll want to conduct a radon test as well; some home inspectors offer this service as part of a package deal, but others don't. And if the home is served by well water, you'll need to get a water quality test, which is typically separate from a home inspection.

Do Your Own Home Inspection

In some cities and towns, building permit records are available online or at city hall. It's worth pulling a home's record to see what, if any, building permits have been filed for the property. That can tell you exactly how old the roof is, for example, or precisely when the kitchen was last renovated. If there was clearly some remodeling done, but no permit to accompany it, that tells you something else—that the work may not have been done by a licensed contractor.

THE HOME APPRAISAL

What's This Home Really Worth, Anyway?

If you're using a mortgage to buy your home, your lender will essentially be your co-owner. In that sense, they're just as invested in your home as you are. So before they pony up the cash to pay for your home, your lender will want to make sure that it's a sound investment; they'll require that an independent appraiser assess the home and determine its fair market value before releasing your funds at closing.

Even though it's your lender who requires this step, you're the one who has to pay for the home appraisal. You can expect to pay a few hundred dollars for this service, but you're unlikely to come into contact with the appraiser.

Lenders themselves don't conduct appraisals—the whole point is to get an unbiased opinion from a third party—but your lender can usually arrange for an appraisal on your behalf.

The home appraiser will evaluate the overall condition of the home and verify that it matches its description in the public record. For example, an appraiser may confirm the acreage of the lot or make sure that each room officially recorded as a "bedroom" has a closet and window. The appraiser will then do some serious number crunching, examining recent comparable sales data ("comps") from nearby homes to determine the current fair market value of the home you're purchasing.

FHA Appraisals

Properties financed with an FHA loan must pass a stricter appraisal process, which includes a basic inspection. (It's not a substitute for a home inspection, however.) An FHA appraiser will not only estimate the home's value but will also check that the home meets some basic livability requirements. For example, all the windows must open, close, and lock; all the appliances must be in working order; water must drain away from the foundation; and there can't be any chipping or peeling paint.

If the home appraises for the agreed-upon purchase price or higher—and it will, over 90 percent of the time—then you're in the clear. The appraisal may be used as the basis for your property tax bill going forward, but other than that, you may never have to think about it again.

However, if the appraisal comes in lower than the contract price, you could have a problem. The mortgage you've been approved for was based on a certain home value, so if that number is lowered, it can throw off the rest of the math too.

For example, say you're purchasing a home for $400,000 with a down payment of $20,000. The lender has approved all of this—they're comfortable loaning you $380,000 toward a $400,000 home, for a 95 percent loan-to-value (LTV) ratio. But if the appraiser determines the home's market value to be $375,000, suddenly the lender is loaning you more money than the home is even worth. That's not what they signed up for.

HOW TO HANDLE A LOW APPRAISAL

There are a number of reasons that an appraisal may come in below the purchase price, but it's most likely to happen in a hot market. Since most real estate sales aren't finalized for thirty to sixty days after an offer is accepted, there's some built-in lag time in the data that appraisers use—and prices can jump quite a bit in just a month or two.

For example, imagine a four-bedroom home that's listed for $400,000 in March. It goes under agreement quickly for $410,000, as the spring market starts to heat up. By the time the sale closes at the end of May, similar homes in the area are selling for $425,000 or more—but the most recent "comp" would suggest a value of $410,000. A good appraiser should be aware of local market trends and factor price acceleration into their assessment, but a fast-rising market does complicate things.

If your appraisal comes in too low, here are some of your options.

Make Up the Difference in Cash

The simplest way to overcome a low appraisal is to make up the difference in cash. In the earlier example, if you were initially approved for a mortgage with a 95 percent loan-to-value ratio, the lender would still typically loan you 95 percent of the appraised value at the agreed-upon interest rate; you'd simply have to make up the difference in cash.

So where before you were approved for a $380,000 loan on a $400,000 house, if the appraisal came in at $375,000, the lender would only let you borrow 95 percent of that, or $356,250—meaning you'd have to increase your down payment from $20,000 to $43,750. Unfortunately, as a first-time buyer, it's unlikely that you've got an extra twenty grand just floating around.

Negotiate a Lower Price

If your offer included an appraisal contingency, you can take this opportunity to negotiate a lower price with the seller. That may mean dropping the price down to the appraised value or splitting the difference. But either way, the seller would have to take the hit or share some of the burden with you.

Depending on the market, a seller may be willing to do this to ensure that the sale goes through. After all, you're both pretty far along in the process to give up now, and any other buyer with a mortgage would probably run into the same issue once it's time for their appraisal.

Get a Second Opinion

Ask to see a copy of the appraisal, and if you think the appraiser is just plain wrong, you can ask your lender how to appeal the appraisal through a Reconsideration of Value (ROV).

Typically you'll need a reason to justify an appeal—maybe you notice that the appraiser got some facts wrong, or included a battered old house down the block as a comparable sale. In the ROV, you'll provide evidence to make your case. Make note of any errors, and supply your own set of comps that would justify a higher appraised value. If your agent knows of pending home sales nearby that would confirm a higher price, that information can also be used in an appeal.

You could also ask about getting a second appraisal from a different company—though there's no guarantee the lender will agree to this, and you'd have to foot the bill or split it with the seller.

Walk Away

Finally, as long as you included the appraisal contingency in your offer, you can simply walk away from the home sale if the appraised value comes in too low and you can't find a way to bridge the gap.

To call that a disappointing outcome would be an understatement, but it could be a blessing in disguise. If an independent professional determines that you were about to drastically overpay for a home, there's a chance they're right.

PURCHASING HOME INSURANCE

Protecting Your Biggest Investment

You're about to spend hundreds of thousands of dollars on a home. You wouldn't want that money to *literally* go up in smoke. And neither does your lender, who's footing most of the bill. So they'll require you to provide proof of homeowner's insurance (called the binder) before releasing the funds necessary to close on your home. But even if it weren't required as part of your mortgage, homeowner's insurance is a must-have.

SHOPPING FOR INSURANCE

Give yourself at least a couple of weeks before closing to secure a homeowner's policy, since not having one could delay the closing and even mess up the sale. As mentioned in Chapter 5, you can start with your auto insurer if you're happy with them; they'll likely give you a discount if you have multiple policies with them.

However, it's still wise to get a couple of other quotes and compare prices, coverage, and customer satisfaction. Check out ratings from Consumer Reports and J.D. Power to see which insurers provide the best claims service in your region; the last thing you need after enduring a house fire or other disaster is to be fighting with your insurance company over an unpaid claim.

You can solicit a handful of quotes yourself from various insurers or work with an independent agent who's free to shop around on your behalf. You can find an independent agent in your area through the Independent Insurance Agents and Brokers of America at IndependentAgent.com, but your real estate agent or lender may also be able to recommend one to you. You can also shop for home insurance on comparison sites such as Insure.com or NetQuote.com.

Some top-rated insurance companies don't sell policies through comparison sites, however. For example, USAA and Amica issue policies only through their own in-house agents or websites. (Furthermore, USAA is only available to members of the military or their family members.)

WHAT KIND OF COVERAGE DO YOU NEED?

Unlike car insurance, some level of which is required in most states, you don't *legally* need to carry home insurance if you own your home outright. But to leave your most valuable asset uninsured would be borderline bananas. If you do have a mortgage, your lender will most certainly demand a minimum amount of coverage.

Required Perils and Liability

Most lenders will require that your homeowner's policy protect against the usual battery of hazards, called "required perils." These include fire, lightning, hail, theft, vandalism, frozen or burst pipes, falling objects, snow- or ice-related damage, and other risks. You'll also need some amount of liability coverage, in the event that someone is injured on your property and sues you.

Replacement Value

Most experts recommend covering your home to its full replacement value—that is, the amount it would cost to rebuild it exactly as it is today (but new). Because let's face it: If a fire destroys your home, and you need to rebuild from scratch, you don't want 80 percent of a home—you want the whole thing.

Plus, in all likelihood, the full replacement cost of your home is actually *less* than what you're paying for it now, because the value of the land is baked into the sale price. For example, even if you're paying $400,000 for a house, it may only cost $250,000 to rebuild it from scratch, as long as you've still got the land beneath it. Your insurance agent can help you estimate this cost (including the price of replicating custom millwork or other valuable architectural details, which can raise the premium).

Home Insurance for Condos

As a condominium owner, you'll automatically have some coverage through your association's "master insurance" policy, which is included in the condo fee. However, that policy covers the building as a whole and any common areas. You'll still need a separate HO6 condo policy to insure against damage to the interior of your unit and to your belongings, as well as liability coverage should any visitors hurt themselves in your unit. Fortunately, this is usually a lot cheaper than a typical homeowner's policy on a single-family house.

Floods and Other Disasters

Unfortunately, there are a lot of things a typical home insurance policy doesn't cover. Chief among them is flooding. While your homeowner's policy will generally reimburse you for water damage caused by a burst water pipe, or even from rain that finds its way into a crack in the wall, once that rain hits the ground, it's considered a flood, and that requires extra coverage.

In low-lying areas that the Federal Emergency Management Agency (FEMA) has designated as prone to flooding, your lender will require you to purchase flood insurance through the National Flood Insurance Program. Even if it's not required, you may wish to get flood coverage if you're near a floodplain or close to a body of water. Flood insurance rates are regulated and subsidized but are still expensive if you're in a high-risk area, averaging about $700 a year.

A standard homeowner's policy may not protect you from some other hazards, such as earthquakes. In areas where earthquakes are more common, you may be required (or simply want) to get an endorsement on the policy—essentially an add-on—that provides earthquake coverage for an extra charge.

Choose Your Deductible

The other decision to make when shopping for home insurance is how big a deductible you want. A deductible is the amount of damage over which your insurance kicks in; for example, if a storm causes $10,000 in damage, and your deductible is $1,000, you'd pay the first $1,000 and your insurance company would kick in $9,000.

The standard deductible is typically $500 or $1,000, but choosing a higher deductible will lower your insurance premium.

TITLE INSURANCE, ATTORNEYS, AND OTHER ODDS AND ENDS

Get Yourself Ready for Closing

At this point in the process, you're probably thinking about paint colors and room arrangements, not title insurance. But with so many moving parts to a home purchase, a lot of things need to happen between the time your offer is accepted and the time you take ownership of your home, even beyond arranging a home inspection and finding insurance.

Some of this occurs behind the scenes, orchestrated by your lender. Your real estate agent, meanwhile—the quarterback of your home purchase team—will help make sure you're aware of your responsibilities and are staying on track to meet any deadlines. Still, it's good to know what to expect from the hectic weeks ahead. Here are some of the things you'll need to do in between packing for the move and looking at paint swatches.

Finalize Your Loan

In addition to the appraisal, your lender may ask you for one more round of recent pay stubs, balance statements, or other financial documentation. Make sure they've got everything they need to finalize your mortgage. If you receive a revised loan estimate, and something in it has changed from the earlier estimate, make sure you understand why.

Hire a Title Company or Attorney

In most states, either a title company's settlement agent, an escrow agent, or a real estate attorney will handle the title search and other mechanics of the home purchase transaction. Your lender can probably arrange much of this for you, but it can be well worth shopping around for the best prices. You could shave up to $500 off your closing costs, according to the Consumer Financial Protection Bureau.

Consult your loan estimate to see which service providers you're allowed to shop around for and which ones you're stuck with. Remember that you also have the option of hiring the closing attorney (or your own separate lawyer) to review the sales contract, mortgage, promissory note, and other legal documents on your behalf.

Schedule Your Closing

Even if your sale agreement specifies a day for closing, you'll need to schedule a time and place to sign all the paperwork with a notary public and officially close the sale.

Write down who will be handling the closing and when and where it will take place. Ask exactly what you need to bring with you that day—for example, you'll need to show identification such as a driver's license or passport, and you may be asked to bring your down payment in the form of a cashier's check, which you can get from your bank.

Virtual Closing

Most real estate closings still happen in person, with all signatures certified by a notary. During the 2020–21 pandemic, however, virtual closings conducted through video conferencing platforms and using electronic signatures became more commonplace. Even in a traditional closing, some documents can be signed securely online ahead of time to speed things up, with no notarization required.

Get Your Down Payment On Deck

As closing nears, you'll want to make sure your down payment funds are in your checking account and ready to be disbursed when the time comes. If you need to transfer savings from a different bank or withdraw funds from a retirement account, don't wait until the last minute, since it can take a few days for those transfers to go through.

Beware of Wire Fraud

In a devastating but all-too-common real estate scam, home buyers receive an urgent email, text, or phone call that appears to be from their real estate agent, urging them to wire their down payment money to a different account just before closing, due to a last-minute change. Be on the lookout for such scams as your closing day nears.

Never wire money to a strange account, as it's nearly impossible to recover wired funds. Discuss the closing procedure with your agent in person and in detail ahead of time; if there's any change to the process you discussed, make sure you confirm it in person or with a fresh phone call to your Realtor. (Don't just call or email back the source of the message, as their contact info may be masked to look like it's coming from your agent.)

Transfer Your Utilities

As closing nears, you'll want to make arrangements to transfer utility services at the property into your name. Even if you're not planning to move in right away, it's important to have heat and electric service turned on in case of emergencies (or to keep pipes from freezing). Call the utility companies to alert them to the sale, and give them a date to transfer the service into your name.

THE FINAL WALK-THROUGH

Reviewing Closing Documents and Dealing with Any Last-Minute Negotiations

You're almost there. Closing is just days away, and the pieces are all falling into place. There are just a couple of last-minute things to attend to—including taking a final look at your mortgage paperwork and the home itself before you officially become a homeowner.

REVIEW THE CLOSING DISCLOSURE

At least three business days before closing (by law), you'll receive a closing disclosure form. Ask your lender, title agent, or closing attorney if this document will come by email, postal mail, or some other means, and be on the lookout for it.

When you receive the closing disclosure form, make sure everything looks accurate. Check the spelling of your name, confirm the basic mortgage details, and compare the final dollar amounts to those in your most recent loan estimate. Some minor cost adjustments are not uncommon as estimates become finalized, but if any of the numbers have changed significantly, make sure you understand why. (A good shortcut to see whether your loan got more expensive is to compare the annual percentage rate, or APR, which includes both the interest rate and fees.)

When you ask about the closing disclosure, you can also request advance copies of some important closing documents, like the mortgage (or deed of trust), the deed, and the promissory note. It's a good idea to review these ahead of time, before any closing-day jitters set in. This also allows you time to have a real estate attorney look over the documents on your behalf if you wish.

CONDUCT A FINAL WALK-THROUGH

Just before the closing—typically the morning of or the night before—you'll have one more chance to inspect the property before taking ownership. The purpose of the final walk-through is to make sure the home is in the same or better condition as when you agreed to buy it, and that any repairs you negotiated after the home inspection have indeed been completed. Bring your agent and a trusted friend or family member; the seller should not be present, since you don't want to feel any pressure from them.

It sounds like a formality, and hopefully it will be, but the final walk-through is a critical step that shouldn't be skipped or rushed. Take your time exploring the home, testing all the light switches, faucets, and outlets, making sure all the appliances, exhaust fans, and HVAC systems work, and checking for things like dents in the wall or cracked window panes that weren't there before. It's probably been a few weeks since the home inspection, and that's more than enough time for the seller (or their moving crew) to have broken a closet door by accident, or for the dishwasher to have sprung a leak.

If the home inspection revealed any problems that the seller agreed to fix before closing, now is the time to make sure those repairs were in fact completed, and done in a professional manner.

It's also important to make sure the seller has actually moved out and removed all of their personal belongings. That includes garbage, junk in the garage or basement, boxes in the attic, and anything else that isn't supposed to be left behind.

"Good" Junk

Some seller souvenirs can be useful, though you're under no obligation to accept them—for example, leftover paint that matches the bathroom walls may be handy if you need to patch a spot later on, and a drawer full of appliance manuals could prove helpful. But don't let the seller saddle you with a heap of broken air conditioners or an ugly old couch that was too big to move.

While you don't want any extra surprises, you also want to make sure everything that was supposed to be included in the sale is still there. Make sure the seller didn't take the refrigerator with them (or replace it with a cheaper model) if it was supposed to remain with the home.

What to Do If You Find Problems

The final walk-through is not the same as a home inspection. This isn't the time to get fussy about the age or condition of the furnace when it's no different than it was a month ago. But if the seller agreed to replace a rotting stair tread or broken faucet and has yet to do so, they're in breach of the purchase agreement. If you find new damage, missing appliances, or other unkept promises, the seller needs to meet the obligations set forth in the sales contract, and fast—or you need to work with them to negotiate an acceptable alternative.

That may mean delaying the closing by a few days, to give the seller time to fix any problems. Or it may just come down to cash. The seller could agree to lower the price by the cost of any repairs that weren't made, for example, or to put some of the money from the sale into an escrow account to pay for a junk removal service. Your agent will negotiate these terms with the seller's agent on your behalf, and write the new terms into the agreement.

You're both so close to the finish line that neither party will want to jeopardize the sale, and that deadline pressure should help pave the way to an agreement. But if the seller refuses to hold up their end of the bargain—if the home is not in the condition stipulated in the purchase agreement—you can still walk away from the sale without losing your earnest money.

CLOSING TIME

Congratulations, Homeowner!

Today's the big day: the closing. It's ironic that something as objectively boring as signing forms in an office for hours on end could generate so much nervous energy, but you'll probably feel some jitters, and that's expected. This is a big deal.

Gather the things your lender or closing agent instructed you to bring to the closing: a form of identification, the balance of your down payment and closing costs (usually in the form of a bank cashier's check or proof of wire transfer), and maybe a checkbook for any last-minute expenses. Then take a deep breath, crack your knuckles, and stretch your wrist, because you've got a lot of papers to sign today.

Some of the contracts you'll sign are between you and the lender; others are between you and the seller. You're going to see and sign some of the documents you may have reviewed in advance, such as your mortgage or deed of trust and the promissory note. Be prepared, as these contain some daunting legal language, like how the bank can foreclose on your home if you don't pay your mortgage. You'll get your initial escrow statement, if you're paying real estate taxes and insurance through an escrow account. You'll also be asked to sign a battery of other forms and disclosures that are required by state, local, or federal law.

It's a lot. You've never seen so many forms in your life.

By this point, you've been patiently waiting to make this home your own for weeks. As tempting as it may be to just sign whatever comes your way to get this last step over with, take your time. Your agent should be there with you, as will your loan officer; ask them, or the closing attorney, to explain anything that you don't understand.

The seller and the seller's agent will also be in attendance, which may make you feel under pressure. Still, don't hurry. This is your last chance to back out of the biggest purchase of your life; you could still simply put down the pen and walk away, though at this point it would probably cost you your earnest money deposit and some of your lender fees.

A Brief Reprieve

By the time you close on your home, both you and your bank account will probably feel pretty drained. The good news is, you'll generally have more than a full month before your first mortgage payment is due. For example, if you close on July 20, your first mortgage payment wouldn't be due until September 1.

Make sure anything you sign matches your expectations, and ask for an explanation if it doesn't. This is the time to catch and fix any errors. Because once you put pen to paper, and the deed is legally recorded at the county registry, it becomes a lot harder to fix even a minor typo.

When the final *i* is dotted and every last *t* is crossed, the seller will hand over the keys to you. And then?

Exhale. Smile. Celebrate. You're a homeowner now. You probably have a million things to do—like move, for starters. But if you wanted to, you could go straight over to your new home and roller skate around the empty rooms, nap on the kitchen counters, or paint your name on the walls. It's all yours, and nobody's going to stop you. Congratulations!

Chapter 10

Moving, Renovations, and Homeownership

Well, *that* was a doozy! What a wild few months, huh? But now you can just sit back, relax, and enjoy your new home....er, just kidding. In fact, the weeks ahead could be even busier still.

You've got the keys to your new home, but it's not exactly "home" yet—at least, not until you schlepp all of your worldly possessions across the threshold and spend the night. And before you endure the headaches and backaches of moving, there may be some home improvements you want to attend to. In this final chapter, we'll discuss tips to simplify packing and moving in, as well as some pointers on hiring contractors and maintaining your new home.

TIPS FOR PACKING AND HIRING MOVERS

"I Like to Move It, Move It," Said No One, Ever, While Carrying a Sofa Through a Doorway

There's no two ways around it: Moving is a royal pain in the neck (and back and shoulders). Whether you do it all yourself or hire professionals, it's bound to be a stressful experience.

You can try to dilute that stress by moving in stages over the course of a week or more, or take a rip-off-the-bandage approach and get it all done in one fell swoop. (Though you may not have much choice in the matter, depending on when you close on your home and whether you have a deadline—such as an expiring lease—to move out of your present living quarters.)

Packing and moving are the two main stages to any move—the first can be mentally exhausting, the other physically demanding—but you can hire professional help for either step. The more effort you invest in packing well, the easier the actual move will be. If your possessions are still scattered about on moving day, it will be that much harder to move them, but many hands can make quick work of well-packed boxes of books, clothes, and kitchenware.

That's not to say it will be easy. If you're only moving boxes of personal items and a handful of larger furnishings—say, a bed, a couch, a table, and a dresser—you can probably coerce a few friends into helping you out. But if you've been living in the same place for a couple of years or more, there's a good chance you've got more stuff than you realize. If you're migrating a full two-bedroom apartment's worth of furniture down two flights of stairs, consider sparing yourself and your friends a hernia and hiring some pros to help, at least for the biggest, heaviest items.

PLANNING, PACKING, AND MOVING

Getting all of your possessions from one place to another is no easy task. Here are some tips to get through your move without losing any of your stuff (including your sanity).

Book Your Move at Least Thirty Days in Advance

As soon as you have a solid move-in date, call to reserve a moving crew or truck. Rental trucks and vans can sell out or skyrocket in price due to surging demand, and reputable moving companies fill up fast during the busiest summer months. You don't want to be stuck scrambling for a truck or a moving crew at the last minute.

Save Money by Moving on a Weekday in the Middle of the Month

Unsurprisingly, weekend days are the busiest times for moving companies, as are the first and last weeks of the month. Whether you're renting a trailer or truck or hiring a moving crew, you'll usually have the easiest time booking your move on a weekday in the middle of the month, and score better rates to boot.

Consult Reviews and Referrals

Online reviews are a good starting point to research movers—although, due to the high-stress nature of moving, even a solid company is bound to have a complaint or two. If your friends had a good or bad experience with a recent move, ask them for details. Avoid a place that overbooked and left your friends stranded without a moving van. Alternatively, if they had a great experience with a particular mover, call that company and request the very same crew members if possible.

Start Packing Early

Moving experts agree: Don't wait until the last minute, then spend the day before (or the morning of!) your move frantically shoving things into boxes and garbage bags. Once you have a move date, start chipping away at the task ahead, packing a few boxes a day. Taking a room-by-room approach can help you make steady progress without getting overwhelmed.

Invest in a packing tape dispenser and start gathering and saving any newspaper (for dishes), Bubble Wrap, and cardboard boxes that you come across; liquor and grocery stores often have free boxes to spare. Even if you're not a customer, moving companies may be able to give you some free boxes and other once-used packing supplies they can no longer sell.

Declutter and Donate

Whether you're doing it yourself or paying for pros, the less stuff you take with you, the easier (and cheaper) your move will be. So take this opportunity to go through your possessions with an eye toward ruthless minimalism.

Are there clothes in your closet or dresser that you haven't worn in over two years? Donate them to a charitable organization. Are there boxes in the basement still taped up from the last time you moved? You clearly don't need whatever's inside them—donate anything useful, and toss the rest. Is your storage container drawer a chaotic tornado of mismatched bowls and lids? Pick your favorites to come with you, and donate or toss the others.

Allow Pros to Pack Fragile Items

If you've hired movers, you can save some time and money by packing easy stuff yourself, such as clothes, books, and dishes. But you may want to enlist the pros to pack anything breakable. They have the experience and materials to do it properly, and any replacement coverage they offer for broken items could be voided if you pack the box yourself.

Label Everything

Do your moved-in self a favor: As you pack, label each box with its destination and contents (e.g., "Kitchen—Pots"). If you've hired a moving service, take photos of furniture so you have proof of its original condition in the event anything is damaged. And before you wave goodbye to all of your belongings, make an inventory of what's going in the truck—for example, nine boxes of kitchen items, two sofas, one coffee table, and so on.

Deconstruct Heavy or Bulky Items

Particularly if you and your friends will be lugging everything onto the truck yourselves, break down big items into smaller, lighter-weight components whenever possible. For example, remove the drawers from dressers and desks, and unscrew a table's legs to make it less awkward going down stairs (and put the hardware in a sealed plastic bag taped to the tabletop).

Keep Valuables with You (and Toiletries Too)

Take your most valuable, irreplaceable items in your own car. This includes things like jewelry, family heirlooms, old photographs, musical instruments, passports, important documents, and cash. Movers recommend that customers transport houseplants themselves, as the dark, stiflingly hot, bouncing back of a moving truck is hardly a happy environment for a potted plant.

It's also smart to pack the equivalent of a carry-on bag or "open first" box filled with toiletries, medications, chargers, linens, and a fresh change of clothes for your first day in your new home.

Is It Worth It to Hire Help?

Wondering what it would cost to hire professional movers? The website Moving .com has a cost estimator based on how big your home is and how far away you're moving. Hiring pros to move the contents of a two-bedroom apartment from San Francisco to San Diego, for example, would cost between $1,371 and $1,715. (Adding full packing services would raise the price to between $2,144 and $2,746.) Renting your own truck to move the same distance, meanwhile, would cost about half that—an average of $750, according to Move.org, including gas.

DO YOU NEED MOVING INSURANCE?

Moving companies generally offer a couple of different levels of coverage in the event that your belongings are accidentally broken or misplaced during the move.

The most basic valuation coverage—which, by law, is included in the price of your move—will reimburse you for lost or broken items at a rate of 30 cents per pound for an in-state move, or 60 cents per pound for interstate moves.

That means you'd get $60 in compensation if interstate movers were to break your 100-pound kitchen table. But if your 20-pound Ultra HD TV was damaged on a cross-town move, you'd receive just $6. If you've ever weighed your laptop or favorite coat, you'll recognize that this coverage generally won't reimburse you for the true value of a lost or damaged item.

Most movers also offer full-value protection for an additional cost. With this coverage in place, the mover must repair, replace, or reimburse you for a broken or lost item—excluding anything of extraordinary value (worth over $100 a pound). That's why, even with this coverage in place, it's still wise to transport valuables yourself.

Full-value protection has other limitations too: It generally doesn't cover any items you packed yourself, and it doesn't protect against natural disasters—for example, if a thunderstorm soaks the box with your computer in it. For full protection, you can opt for third-party moving insurance from an insurer (a product that moving companies aren't legally permitted to sell). This will supplement the mover's valuation coverage and add protection against road accidents and weather.

If you have renter's insurance or a homeowner's policy, you may have some limited coverage as well. For example, if an item is stolen off the moving truck, your renter's policy might offer partial coverage. Check with your insurance provider, however, as homeowner's and renter's policies vary quite a bit in how they handle items once they're outside of your home—and most don't cover simple breakage.

Regardless of what level coverage you have, whether it's bare bones or full replacement value, you'll need to document what you're moving if you want to be reimbursed for anything that goes missing or breaks. Your phone is your friend here: Take pictures of everything, before and after it's packed. For truly valuable items, snap a photo of the model number to help authenticate its value. With any luck, you can simply go back and delete these pictures a few days from now, while sitting on your undamaged couch in your new home.

WHICH RENOVATIONS TO DO BEFORE YOU MOVE IN—AND WHICH CAN WAIT

This Canvas Won't Be Blank for Long

Unless you just bought a brand-new or gut-remodeled home, there may be some home improvement projects you're keen on making. Your home inspection report may have even outlined a prioritized list of suggested repairs or upgrades.

It's always easier to renovate a home when it's empty. There's no furniture in the way, nobody's bothered when the water or electricity is turned off, and cleanup is a piece of cake. A vacant home is something of a blank canvas.

However, what's *not* always easy is paying for a home remodeling project after you just ponied up thousands of dollars in down payment money. Nor is it always feasible to continue paying rent on one home for several more months while paying for a mortgage and a contractor on another.

Renovations to Tackle Now, If Possible

If there's work that you definitely want to do to your new home, and you have the financial ability and time to get the work done before moving in, then by all means, go for it. It will be easier on you and your contractor alike if there's no furniture, paintings, or pets in the way while they're breaking open walls and ripping up floorboards, and it will feel great to move into a home that's everything you imagined.

However, time and money are two big "ifs" for most first-time home buyers. So in the more likely scenario that you need to prioritize your early home improvement spending, here are some of the things best taken care of before you move in.

- **Safety issues:** First things first, make sure you address any safety concerns before moving in, or as soon as possible upon occupancy. Ensure there are enough working smoke alarms and carbon monoxide detectors installed, get any broken steps or deck railings replaced, and address any immediate electrical or fire hazards.

- **Leaks:** Water is a home's worst enemy, so a leaking roof or pipe should be at the top of your to-do list. If rain is getting inside the home, no other improvement you make will matter, because all of it could just end up soggy and water damaged.

- **Painting:** Interior painting is a lot easier to do in a vacant home, when you don't have to worry about dripping paint on couches or lamps, and you don't have to sleep amid the fumes. Plus, painting is quite cheap if you do it yourself, so you may want to take a stab at this before moving in. (However, if you don't get a chance to, it's still simple enough to paint the walls, trim, and ceiling in an occupied home, especially if you take it one room at a time. You can also purchase low- or no-VOC paints that don't release such harmful fumes.)

- **Refinishing or installing new floors:** It's not *impossible* to refinish the hardwood floors in a fully furnished, occupied home, but it's a *lot* harder to pull off. Not only does the contractor need the floors completely free of furniture; the process involves a tremendous amount of dust and smelly coats of polyurethane as well. However, if you have a major remodel planned for the future, it's best to wait on new or refinished flooring until after that work is completed.

- **Bathroom remodel (if it's the only bathroom):** It won't kill you to live with a working but dated bathroom for a couple of years. But if the bathroom you want to remodel is the only one in the home, it may be worth renovating now, while you still have somewhere else to live (and shower). A full bathroom renovation can take about four and a half weeks, according to *The Spruce*, and that's a long time to go without a working toilet or tub.
- **Plumbing upgrades:** If you're hoping to replace your home's ancient heating or water pipes, you're generally going to need to open up the walls to do so. That's a big, messy job that's best done when you're not around—not to mention the fact that living without running water, even for a few days, isn't particularly convenient.

Condo Owners Spend Half As Much on Home Improvement

Owners of single-family homes spend an average of $3,600 a year on remodeling and repairs, according to research by the Joint Center for Housing Studies at Harvard University, compared to $1,800 spent by condo owners.

Renovations That Can Wait

There's a chance that just about all of your home improvement plans have to take a backseat to more urgent expenses. The following projects can generally be put on hold for a while.

- **Exterior work:** Aside from important safety or urgent structural issues, most exterior work can wait until you're good and ready.

Projects like siding, decks, replacement windows, landscaping, or paving a driveway can all be done after you've moved in, and will present only a minor inconvenience during construction.

- **Cosmetic improvements to otherwise functional spaces:** We all want our dream kitchen, and it's definitely preferable to have it ready and waiting for you when you first move in rather than living through a six-week kitchen remodel with your microwave and refrigerator crammed into the dining room. However, as long as the current kitchen is functional—with a working stove and sink—you can probably make it work until you're financially ready for a full renovation. In fact, living with the existing kitchen for a while (or any room destined for a remodel) may grant you some valuable insight into what you like about the present layout and how it could be improved.

- **Electrical upgrades:** It's easier to replace outdated wiring when the walls are already opened up, of course. But electricians are surprisingly deft at snaking wires through wall cavities if they need to. As long as there's no urgent safety hazard, this is an improvement you can wait on.

- **Equipment upgrades:** Replacing a boiler, furnace, or hot water heater can be done just about any time. That said, it's always preferable to upgrade aging home systems on your timetable, when you've had some time to plan and budget for it. If your furnace doesn't look like it will make it through another winter, plan to get it replaced on a normal weekday in late summer as opposed to a frantic Sunday night during a January snowstorm.

GENERAL TIPS ON HOME IMPROVEMENTS

Planning and Paying for Repairs and Remodeling

Now that you're the proud owner of your own home, you're invariably going to end up doing some maintenance or hiring a contractor, whether it's to install a shelf, fix a faulty outlet, or put your personal stamp on the kitchen design. Here are some tips for planning future renovations and working with contractors.

Try to Be Proactive, Not Reactive

It's both easier and cheaper to perform a planned upgrade to your water heater on a weekday afternoon than it is to pay for an emergency replacement while hosting houseguests over Memorial Day weekend. Preparing for inevitable equipment failures allows you time to research online reviews and rebate programs, prepare for a brief water or electricity outage during installation, and save up money to do the work on your terms and schedule. Waiting until a problem escalates to emergency status is expensive and stressful.

Use your home inspection report and its punch list of issues or suggested repairs as a blueprint for the improvements and upgrades you may want to make. If you can keep up your down payment saving habits, set aside some money for any anticipated projects on the horizon. Emergencies will flare up regardless—but the more of them you can tackle on your own terms, the better.

Most home improvement spending can be split into two categories: upkeep and repairs, such as a new furnace or roof; and more glamorous, discretionary projects, like interior remodeling. Try to get on top of the maintenance and repairs before blowing your budget on a new kitchen—even though the latter is, admittedly, way more fun.

Find Your Go-To Tradespeople

For the minor emergencies that do happen, as well as maintenance services you'll need every year or two, it's good to develop trusted relationships with some local tradespeople. Ask other homeowners in your area whom they turn to for basic plumbing, HVAC, and carpentry work, as well as for landscaping and gutter cleaning services. Once again, online reviews are a good starting point, but referrals from neighbors can be even more valuable.

Get Multiple Quotes

This goes without saying, but you should always solicit at least three estimates for a major remodeling project. Contractors may offer wildly different prices for the same job—not just based on the cost of the work and materials but also on what it's worth to them. For example, one may underbid just to get the job (and you may get what you pay for), while others may intentionally overbid because they're already too booked up (but could push other jobs aside for the right price).

But you're not just evaluating contractors on price. Ask how they would approach the project, how much of the work would be hired out to subcontractors, whether they'll take care of permits and inspections, and what the payment schedule and project timeline would be (never pay more than a deposit upfront). Ask to see proof of their insurance—they should have both liability and worker's compensation coverage—and check that their contractors' license is current.

A good contractor should provide you with a detailed, itemized estimate that clearly explains the scope of the work, the cost of various materials and labor, and what you'll be paying and when. For bigger jobs, like a new kitchen or bathroom, it can be worth contacting references or past clients. Then ask yourself: Would you feel comfortable with this person and their crew entering your house every day? Do they, and their portfolio of past projects, inspire confidence?

Pull Permits

Not all home improvement projects require you to pull a building permit with your city or town, but quite a few of them do. Minor cosmetic work and appliance swaps don't typically require a permit—for example, you generally won't need a permit to paint your walls, replace a leaky faucet or dishwasher, or hang cabinets in the kitchen. But anytime you alter the structure, plumbing, or electrical system in your home, you will probably need to get a building permit.

A good contractor should take care of this for you; be very wary if they suggest bypassing the permit process. And even if you're doing the work yourself, don't skip this step. It may seem like an unnecessary hassle and expense, but construction inspections are designed to protect you—to make sure your new wiring is up to code and not a fire hazard, for instance, and to ensure the plumber didn't rig something that will work for a few years but ultimately fail.

Getting a permit means your improvements are legal and legit, not half-baked, slap-dash fixes—which will matter to future home buyers. What's more, if local inspectors pass by your home and see a renovation in progress without a permit, they can put a stop to the project, fine you, delay construction for months, or even force you to undo already completed work for inspection.

Don't Be Afraid to DIY

We live in a golden age of information—there are free how-to videos and tutorials available online for just about every home fix conceivable. Many home improvement projects are simple enough for a beginner to handle with a bit of guidance, even if it may take you four times longer than a professional to complete them.

Just remember one of the golden rules of construction: Measure twice, cut once. Check and then double-check what you're doing before putting holes in your walls or ceilings. This even applies to something as simple as hanging a picture in the bathroom. A poorly placed nail or screw can go right into a water pipe or electrical wire if you're not careful. (A stud finder can help you locate and avoid the mechanical workings behind a wall.) Always remember to shut off the power or water supply before working with electricity or plumbing—and then double-check that it's off.

Consider Resale Value

Unless you're flipping a house for profit or getting it ready to sell, the home improvements you make should be for your enjoyment, not for anyone else's. That said, knowing that you'll likely recoup at least half of what you invest in a kitchen remodel when it comes time to sell can help soften the sting of its $40,000 price tag. So if you're trying to decide which remodeling project to do first, you could look at the ones most likely to improve your home's value in the long run.

Some of the projects with the best return on investment, according to *Remodeling Magazine*'s 2021 Cost Versus Value Report, are replacing garage doors (93.8 percent of the project cost recovered at resale), a minor kitchen remodel (72.2 percent), exterior siding (68.3 percent to 69.4 percent), and adding a wood or composite deck (63.2 percent to 65.8 percent).

How Much Does a New Kitchen Cost?

Costs will vary by region and market fluctuations, such as lumber prices, but here's how much American homeowners paid, on average, for common home improvements in 2020, according to *HomeAdvisor*'s 2021 True Cost Report:

- Bathroom remodel: $13,401
- Kitchen remodel: $35,313
- Roof replacement: $9,375
- Exterior painting: $3,291
- Deck or porch: $7,994
- New fencing: $2,991
- In-ground pool: $49,245

Consider Projects That Pay for Themselves

Some home improvements actually pay for themselves, and not just at resale. Adding solar panels to your roof, for example, or improving your home's insulation and energy efficiency can save you money every month going forward. Some federal, state, and local programs offer grants or rebates to help homeowners offset the upfront costs of improving efficiency, so see what's available to you—there may be free money or zero-interest loans available.

Tapping Home Equity

Speaking of loans, are you wondering how on earth people pay for a new kitchen? Well, here's one way: Once you've been in your home for a while, paying down the mortgage principal even as home values rise, you may find yourself with home equity that you can borrow against.

As you remember, home equity is the difference between what you owe on your home and what it's worth—your ownership stake in the home. Lenders will typically let you borrow against that equity for home improvements (or other big expenses) through a home equity loan.

For example, say you bought a $400,000 home using a $360,000 mortgage—your initial equity stake is 10 percent, same as your down payment. After five years, you've paid down your mortgage balance to $330,000, and home prices in your area have increased about 4 percent a year, bringing your home's value to $480,000. That means you now have about $150,000 in home equity.

You can't take out all of that equity—lenders still like you to keep a cushion of at least 20 percent of the home's value, much like their preferred down payment. But now that 80 percent of your home's value is roughly $389,000, and you owe $330,000 on your mortgage, you could potentially take out a home equity loan of up to $59,000, provided your credit and income can support the payments. Even pulling out half that much would put a new kitchen just about within reach.

Home equity loans are essentially second mortgages, and they involve a similar spate of credit checks, income verifications, and closing costs (though they're not as high as those on a primary mortgage). But like mortgages, home equity loans also offer very low interest rates, because your home is used as collateral, and loan terms can be anywhere from five to thirty years.

NEW HOMEOWNER CHECKLIST

A To-Do List for Your First Week of Homeownership

There's a lot to do when you first move into a new home; it's a whirl-wind of hustle, excitement, and possibility. But while you may be understandably focused on wall colors or finding furniture for new rooms you've never had before—or simply figuring out where the nearest grocery store is—don't let these small but important tasks slip through the cracks.

Change Your Address

As soon as you move (or up to three months beforehand), submit a change of address form to the US Postal Service at https://moversguide.usps.com, which will forward any mail from your old address to your new home for six months. That's just a backstop, though—you'll need to actively change your address with everyone from your workplace to your bank to any magazines or services you subscribe to. Start logging into each of your accounts, in order of importance, and change your address in each one.

Set Up Utilities

If you haven't already, call the electric and gas companies to transfer service into your name (and cancel service at your previous address). If your home uses oil or propane for heating, you may need to set up a delivery service; you may receive introductory offer coupons in the mail during your first few months, so take advantage of any good offers you find. Likewise, see what kind of new customer deals are available for Internet service.

Change the Locks

It's always a smart idea to change the locks when you move into a new home, just to be safe—you don't know how many spare keys to your home may still be floating around. Swapping out a lockset is a fairly simple, straightforward project—making it a good introduction to DIY home improvement if you're new to such things—and should only cost you about $50 to $100. If the door has a keyless entry, reprogram the code (and don't use 1-2-3-4 or 1-1-1-1).

The Key to Happiness?

Do yourself a favor if possible and get a matching front and back lockset, so you only need one key for both entrances. Get a couple of extra keys made at the hardware store, and give one to a trusted family member, friend, or neighbor for emergencies.

Deep Clean

Even if the seller left the home fairly tidy, give it a thorough cleaning before you unpack. Wash the floors (and the walls too—it'll help paint adhere better), scrub the empty refrigerator, scour the bathroom tub and tile. It's far easier to clean without anything in the way, and it will feel good to know that you're starting your life in your new home with a literal clean slate.

Start a Home Binder

After signing all those documents at closing, you've now got a whole bunch of important paperwork that needs a safe home. Gather all of your home-related documents into one folder or binder, and keep it in a safe, secure place—but continue adding to it, such as when you get a contractor receipt or an update to your home insurance policy, for example.

Prepare for Emergencies

The time to be googling the closest hospital is not during a health emergency. Think some things through now so you'll be prepared in a crisis later. That includes:

- **Locate and map a route to your nearest or preferred hospital:** Note that traffic patterns may mean a farther-away hospital is easier to get to at certain times of the day.
- **Note emergency numbers:** Don't just assume that your community uses 911. Look up your emergency phone numbers—including police, fire, and poison control—and put them on the refrigerator.
- **Create a fire plan for your family:** Does everyone have multiple exits? Choose a meeting point outside the home so you'll know that everyone made it out safely.
- **Locate your shutoff valves:** If there's a water or gas leak in your home, you want to be able to stop it immediately. Check that every sink and toilet has a nearby water shutoff, and make sure they work. Do the same for gas stoves or dryers. Also find the home's main water, gas, and electric shutoffs. These may all be in the basement, or they could be in different locations throughout and outside the home, but make a mental note of their locations so you can quickly and completely stop a leak.

Start Filling Furniture Gaps

If you're moving from a small apartment or a family member's spare bedroom into a full-sized home, you may need to find some key items of furniture. Remember, you can always upgrade to nicer items as money permits, so don't feel the need to spend your last dollars on a brand-new couch or dining room table.

Ask family members if they have furniture or housewares they're no longer using, and check secondhand stores, online yard sales, and Buy Nothing groups for cookware and wooden items (which present no risk of bedbugs) such as tables, dressers, and chairs.

Keep the Momentum Going

House hunting, applying for mortgages, making offers, closing, moving in…this has probably been an exhausting few months. And at some point, you're going to crash. So for now, ride the wave of adrenaline and excitement that comes from being a new homeowner, and get as much done as you can before you hit the wall.

Unpack every box, put up pictures and decorate, organize the rooms, and get your home as close to your vision as you can while you're on a roll. Because once the inevitable slowdown hits, anything still packed in a moving box is likely to stay that way for the foreseeable future.

HOME MAINTENANCE SCHEDULE

Taking Care of Your Prized Possession

Just as a car needs its oil changed and brake pads replaced from time to time, a home needs regular attention to continue running smoothly for decades to come. Spending a few weekends a year on basic maintenance will help protect your investment and stave off larger, more costly headaches later on. (Condo buyers, you're in luck: Much of this stuff—though not all of it—will probably be taken care of for you.)

Some maintenance is only needed periodically—a septic tank, for example, should be inspected every three years. However, most common home upkeep tasks are annual or semiannual affairs. Handily, the changing seasons create a natural, built-in schedule for you to follow.

SPRING

- If your home has central air or forced-air heat, schedule a semiannual HVAC servicing.
- Clean or replace your HVAC filters, and clean bathroom exhaust fans and the dryer vent (lint buildup can cause a fire).
- Each time you change the clocks to adjust for Daylight Saving Time, check the batteries in your smoke and carbon monoxide detectors.
- Inspect the exterior of your home for any signs of winter damage: Have any shingles come loose? Any cracked or peeling paint? If you'll need a contractor, start planning now for summer jobs.

- Sweep and wash your deck. On wood decks, check how the stain or paint is holding up, and recoat if necessary. Stair treads and decking typically need a fresh coat of stain every one or two years, depending on the conditions they're exposed to; railings can generally go for three years or more before they need a touch-up.

- If you have a sump pump, make sure it's working properly before heavy spring rains put it to the test.

- There's a reason they call it spring cleaning. After spending all winter cooped up indoors, it feels good to open the windows, air out your home, and give everything a thorough wipe down. Wash carpets and cabinets, clean out sink drains, and send the vacuum hose into any nooks and crannies you may skip during regular cleaning.

- Turfgrass likes cool-but-not-freezing weather, so seed your lawn early in the spring if it has bare patches.

- Store your snowblower, if you have one. Wipe it down to remove rock salt, empty or run off the remaining gas in the tank, and lubricate all the moving parts.

- Test out your lawnmower, and sharpen the blade if necessary. (You can use a $10 metal file to sharpen lawn mower and hedge clipper blades, or schedule a tune-up with a small-engine specialist and let them handle it as part of the service.)

- Plant perennials, spread a thin layer of mulch in garden beds, and pull weeds before they get themselves deeply rooted. Vegetable gardens and annuals can be planted after the threat of frost has passed.

- Bring rain barrels out of winter storage and hook them up to your downspouts to harness free rainwater for plants and gardens.

Gas-Free Grass

Electric and battery-powered lawn mowers have come a long way in recent years. They can be just as powerful as most gas mowers, but they run more quietly, need barely any maintenance (there are no spark plugs or carburetors to worry about), release no exhaust, and don't require you to keep gasoline in your garage. If your yard is a half-acre or less, consider going electric.

SUMMER

- If you have window air conditioning units, get them out of storage before the first scorching-hot day. (Carrying heavy appliances down from a stifling attic is no fun.) Check for mold or mildew inside, and give them a good cleaning if necessary. Clean or replace the filter and install the air conditioners before the first heat wave.
- Clean the filters in central and window air conditioning units at least once a month.
- Get in the habit of drawing east- and southeast-facing curtains or shades before you go to bed, so the morning sun doesn't heat up your home as quickly. Then, before midday, draw the shades on the south and southwest sides of the home to lessen the load on your air conditioner.
- Check for signs of insects and rodents, and get ahead of any infestations. If it's more than you can handle, you can hire pest control companies to eradicate a single issue—such as a hornet's nest in the eaves—or to perform ongoing service during peak critter season.

- Summer is a great time for exterior painting. If your siding, trim, deck, or porch needs a fresh coat of protective paint or stain, keep an eye on the forecast and get started when a dry spell hits.
- Make sure you have a kit ready for power outages brought on by summer thunderstorms or brownouts—flashlights, candles, and so on—and that you could find that kit in the dark. If you have a backup battery for phones and other devices, make sure it's fully charged.

FALL

- Get your heating system in shape for the cold. Schedule a semi-annual cleanout for your furnace and HVAC system. If your home is heated with radiators, schedule an annual cleanout and servicing of your boiler. The technician can also inspect and test your radiators for leaky valves.
- Test the batteries in your thermostat if it's not hardwired.
- Rake, rake, rake (or mow). Leaves can create a nice, natural winter mulch around the base of shrubs and plants, but you'll want to avoid a blanket of leaves smothering your lawn. You can, however, grind up a moderate amount of leaves with a mulching lawn mower to naturally fertilize the grass.
- Once all the leaves have fallen, clean your gutters so snowmelt and spring rains can freely drain from the roof. Be extremely careful on the ladder, and hire a pro if your roof is too high for comfort.
- Not too hot and not too cold, fall is a good time for interior painting, since you can open the windows for ventilation. Now is also the time to book contractors for winter projects.

- With cooler weather in store, fall is another good time to reseed your lawn. You can also plant trees, shrubs, and perennials; plant tulip and daffodil bulbs before the ground freezes.
- Before the first freeze, drain your garden hoses and store them for the winter. Shut off the water supply to your outdoor spigots, so they don't freeze and crack. Empty rain barrels and keep them in the garage or basement for the winter so they aren't damaged by extreme temperatures.
- Clean out the caked-on grass from your lawn mower and lubricate the moving parts, then stow it away. Get your snow blower into the ready position. Give it a test run before the first snow flies, and get a tune-up if necessary.
- Once again, when you set the clocks back, check the batteries in your smoke alarms and carbon monoxide detectors.
- Order and stack firewood if you use your fireplace or woodstove.
- Get your chimney(s) inspected and swept if necessary.
- This is a good time to clean your windows inside and out, to wash off summer pollen and allow as much sunlight into your home as possible as daylight starts to dwindle. Once open-window season is behind you, reinstall storm windows if you removed them, seal any drafty crevices with caulk, and swap screens for glass panels in your storm doors.
- Give your home's exterior one final check before you batten down the hatches for winter, making sure there are no gaps, cracks, or damage that could worsen with nasty weather. Call a contractor to inspect or repair any suspected roof or siding damage.

WINTER

- Change your furnace filter as often as recommended throughout the heating season.
- If you have a steam boiler, which has a narrow sight glass to indicate the water level inside the tank, add water as needed to keep it two-thirds full—typically every two to four weeks during the heating season.
- Stock up: If you get heavy snow in your area, stockpile basic supplies in case you're without power or unable to get out during a snowstorm. Pick up a bag of snow melt before the first storm, make sure your snow shovel is still in good shape, and replenish your supply of canned food, water, medications, and other emergency supplies.
- If you want to trim branches on a healthy shade tree (such as an oak or maple) or evergreen (such as a pine or spruce), do it in late winter or very early spring, while the tree is dormant. (Flowering trees, such as dogwoods, should be pruned in late summer.)

Just like that, you've made it through your first year as a homeowner. It's okay if you let a few things slide here and there, but don't allow yourself to fall too far behind on maintenance, especially when it comes to matters of safety.

After all, you're asking a lot of both the structure and spirit of this new home. You're counting on it to protect you—to keep you safe and secure from the elements, yes, but also to shelter you from the stresses and threats of the outside world. To help you store and grow your wealth for years, maybe generations, to come. To serve as a backdrop to the life you've always imagined. It's not just a bunch of walls, windows, and a roof—it's a nest, a bank, and a memory factory.

You've worked hard to make this home your own, and it should be a sanctuary of sorts—a joyful, comfortable space, where you feel at peace and at ease, where you can be your true self and let your guard down. So take care of this place. The more love you show your new home, the more it will love you back.

INDEX

ABOUT THE AUTHOR

Jon Gorey is an award-winning freelance writer covering real estate, home improvement, travel, family, and personal finance. Based in Boston, Jon writes most frequently for *The Boston Globe* and *The Boston Globe Magazine*, as well as his award-winning real estate and home improvement blog, *House & Hammer*. Other bylines include *Apartment Therapy*, *Mommy Poppins*, and *Boston* magazine. Jon has received a dozen awards from the National Association of Real Estate Editors (NAREE), including the President's Gold Award for Best Freelance Collection in 2019.